Developing Clairvoyance:

The Ultimate Guide to Unlocking Your Psychic Gifts and Connecting with the Spiritual World

by Sergio Rijo

AF239049

SERGIO RIJO

DEVELOPING CLAIRVOYANCE

THE ULTIMATE GUIDE TO UNLOCKING YOUR PSYCHIC GIFTS AND CONNECTING WITH THE SPIRITUAL WORLD

DEVELOPING CLAIRVOYANCE: THE ULTIMATE GUIDE TO UNLOCKING YOUR PSYCHIC GIFTS AND CONNECTING WITH THE SPIRITUAL WORLD

First edition. April 13, 2023.

Copyright © 2023 SERGIO RIJO.

ISBN: 979-8215238899

Written by SERGIO RIJO.

Table of Contents

"There are more things in heaven and earth, Horatio, Than are dreamt of in your philosophy."

William Shakespeare

Chapter 1: Introduction to Clairvoyance

Welcome to Developing Clairvoyance: The Ultimate Guide to Unlocking Your Psychic Gifts and Connecting with the Spiritual World. If you are reading this, you are probably curious about clairvoyance and exploring ways to develop your psychic abilities.

In this first chapter, we will dive into the basics of clairvoyance and what it means to develop this powerful gift. We will explore different types of psychic abilities and the benefits of honing your clairvoyant skills.

What is Clairvoyance?

Clairvoyance, which means "clear seeing" in French, is the ability to see beyond the physical realm and gain information through extrasensory perception. This means that clairvoyants can access information that is not available through the five physical senses.

Clairvoyance is a natural ability that we all possess to some extent. However, some individuals have a stronger innate ability than others. Through practice and development, anyone can improve their clairvoyant abilities and unlock their full potential.

Different Types of Psychic Abilities

Clairvoyance is just one of many different types of psychic abilities. Some other common psychic abilities include:

Clairaudience: The ability to hear beyond the physical realm.

Clairsentience: The ability to sense or feel information beyond the physical realm.

Claircognizance: The ability to have a deep knowing or understanding of information beyond the physical realm.

Psychometry: The ability to gain information about an object or person by touching it.

Mediumship: The ability to communicate with spirits of deceased individuals.

Telepathy: The ability to communicate with others through thoughts and emotions.

These are just a few examples of the many different types of psychic abilities that exist. Each individual has a unique combination of these abilities, and with practice, they can learn to harness and develop them.

The Benefits of Developing Clairvoyance

Developing clairvoyance can offer a wide range of benefits, both in your personal life and in your professional life. Here are just a few of the benefits you may experience:

Increased intuition: As you develop your clairvoyant abilities, you will also strengthen your intuition. This can help you make better decisions, trust your gut instincts, and navigate challenging situations with more ease.

Improved communication: Clairvoyants are often able to communicate with others on a deeper level. This can help you connect with people on a more meaningful level, build stronger relationships, and improve your communication skills.

Access to spiritual guidance: As you develop your clairvoyance, you may also begin to receive guidance from the spiritual realm. This can help you gain a deeper understanding of your purpose in life, and offer guidance as you navigate challenges and make important decisions.

Personal growth: Developing your clairvoyant abilities can also help you grow and evolve as a person. You will become more self-aware, gain a deeper understanding of yourself and others, and learn to approach life with more empathy and compassion.

Professional opportunities: Finally, developing your clairvoyant abilities can open up a wide range of professional opportunities. You may be able to offer readings, consultations, or coaching services, or you may find that your enhanced intuition and communication skills help you excel in your current career.

In the next chapter, we will explore the concept of energy and how it relates to clairvoyance. We will dive into the different types of energy and how they affect the body, mind, and spirit. Until then, take some time to reflect on your own psychic abilities and consider what benefits you hope to gain from developing your clairvoyance.

Chapter 2: Understanding Energy

Energy is a term that is used often, but what exactly does it mean? We use the term to describe things like electricity, heat, and light, but what is energy really? In this chapter, we will explore the concept of energy, the different types of energy, and how it affects our bodies.

What is Energy?

Energy is a fundamental concept in physics, but it is also a crucial concept in our everyday lives. At its most basic level, energy is the capacity to do work. In other words, it is what makes things happen. Energy can take many forms, and it can be transferred from one object to another.

The Different Types of Energy

There are many different types of energy, and they can be classified in various ways. One way to classify energy is by the way it is stored or released. For example, potential energy is energy that is stored in an object and is released when the object moves. Kinetic energy, on the other hand, is the energy of motion.

Another way to classify energy is by its source. For example, solar energy comes from the sun, and wind energy comes from the wind. Chemical energy is stored in the bonds between atoms and molecules and is released when those bonds are broken.

How Energy Affects the Body

Energy is essential for life. Our bodies use energy to perform all of the functions that keep us alive, from breathing and circulating blood to thinking and moving. The food we eat is converted into energy that our bodies can use.

The type of energy we consume can have a significant impact on our bodies. For example, consuming too many calories from sugar can lead to weight gain and other health problems. On the other hand, consuming healthy fats and proteins can provide our bodies with the energy they need to function optimally.

Energy also affects our emotional state. We all have experienced feeling tired and lethargic when we don't have enough energy to get through the day. Conversely, when we have an abundance of energy, we feel alert, awake, and ready to take on the world.

In addition to the energy we consume, we also have our own energy fields. This energy field, also known as our aura, surrounds our bodies and is made up of electromagnetic energy. It can be affected by our thoughts, emotions, and environment.

In the context of clairvoyance, energy is also essential. When we receive messages and guidance from the spiritual world, it is through the medium of energy. The energy that we receive is processed by the body and the mind, and it is through this processing that we are able to interpret the messages that we receive.

Understanding energy is a crucial step in developing clairvoyance and other psychic abilities. By understanding the different types of energy and how energy affects the body, we can better understand how to connect with the spiritual world and receive the guidance that we seek.

Chapter 3: Mindfulness and Meditation

In today's fast-paced world, many of us find ourselves constantly on the go, with little time to stop and reflect. Our minds are often overwhelmed with thoughts, worries, and distractions, leaving little room for clarity and intuition. However, with the practice of mindfulness and meditation, we can learn to quiet the mind and develop our clairvoyant abilities.

What is Mindfulness?

Mindfulness is the practice of being present and fully engaged in the current moment, without judgment. It involves paying attention to our thoughts, feelings, and sensations, as well as our surroundings. Mindfulness can be practiced at any time, during any activity, and is a powerful tool for developing clairvoyance.

The Benefits of Mindfulness for Developing Clairvoyance

When we practice mindfulness, we become more aware of our thoughts and emotions. This increased awareness allows us to identify and release any negative or limiting beliefs that may be holding us back from developing our clairvoyant abilities. Mindfulness also helps us to quiet the mind, allowing us to access our intuition and receive guidance from the spiritual realm.

In addition to these benefits, mindfulness has been shown to reduce stress, anxiety, and depression, and improve overall well-being. When we are in a relaxed and peaceful state, we are better able to receive intuitive guidance and connect with our higher selves.

Different Types of Meditation

There are many different types of meditation, each with its own unique benefits. Some popular types of meditation include:

Mindfulness meditation: This involves focusing on the present moment and being fully aware of our thoughts, feelings, and sensations.

Transcendental meditation: This involves repeating a mantra or sound to quiet the mind and access deeper levels of consciousness.

Loving-kindness meditation: This involves cultivating feelings of love, compassion, and gratitude towards ourselves and others.

Chakra meditation: This involves focusing on the seven energy centers of the body, known as chakras, and balancing their energy.

Visualization meditation: This involves visualizing a peaceful scene or desired outcome, and using the power of imagination to manifest it into reality.

Regardless of the type of meditation, the key is to find a technique that resonates with you and commit to a regular practice. Just a few minutes of meditation each day can have a profound impact on your clairvoyant development and overall well-being.

Mindfulness and meditation are powerful tools for developing clairvoyance. By practicing mindfulness, we can become more aware of our thoughts and emotions, and identify any limiting beliefs that may be holding us back. And by practicing meditation, we can quiet the mind, access our intuition, and connect with the spiritual realm. So take some time each day to quiet your mind and tune into your intuition – the benefits are well worth the effort.

Chapter 4: Developing Your Intuition

Intuition is that gut feeling you get when you know something without being able to explain why. It's the instinctual sense that we all possess, but some people have a greater ability to tap into it than others. Intuition is often referred to as the "sixth sense" because it goes beyond the five physical senses that we use to navigate the world around us.

What is intuition?

Intuition is a deep understanding of something that is not immediately apparent. It is a feeling or sense that we have, which is not based on logic or reason. It's often described as a hunch or a gut feeling, and it's a way of knowing that comes from within us.

The benefits of developing intuition

Intuition is a powerful tool that can help us make better decisions in all aspects of our lives. When we develop our intuition, we become more attuned to our inner voice, and we are better able to trust ourselves. This can lead to greater self-confidence and self-esteem.

In addition to the personal benefits, developing our intuition can also help us to be more successful in our professional lives. When we are able to trust our intuition, we are better able to make quick and accurate decisions, which can be particularly beneficial in high-pressure situations.

Techniques for developing intuition

Listen to your gut: The first step in developing your intuition is to learn to listen to your gut. Pay attention to those feelings and hunches that you get, and learn to trust them.

Practice mindfulness: Mindfulness is the practice of being present in the moment, and it can help you to become more attuned to your intuition. Take some time each day to sit quietly and focus on your breath.

Keep a journal: Keeping a journal can help you to recognize patterns and themes in your life. Write down your thoughts and feelings, and look for connections between them.

Trust yourself: Learning to trust yourself is a key part of developing your intuition. Don't second-guess yourself, and don't let the opinions of others sway you from your inner voice.

Practice visualization: Visualization is a powerful tool for developing intuition. Take some time to visualize yourself using your intuition in different situations. Imagine yourself trusting your gut and making confident decisions.

Meditate: Meditation can help you to quiet your mind and connect with your inner voice. There are many different types of meditation, so find one that works for you.

Pay attention to your dreams: Your dreams can be a powerful source of intuition. Keep a dream journal and write down your dreams each morning. Look for patterns and themes in your dreams, and pay attention to any messages that you receive.

Developing your intuition takes time and practice, but it is a skill that can be learned by anyone. When you learn to trust your intuition, you become more confident in your decision-making and more attuned to your inner voice. This can lead to greater success in all aspects of your life.

Intuition is not just a passive feeling or sense that we have, but an active tool that we can use to make better decisions. By following the techniques outlined above, you can begin to tap into your intuition and develop it to its fullest potential.

Developing your intuition is an essential skill for anyone who wants to live a more fulfilling and successful life. By learning to trust your intuition, you can make better decisions, become more confident in yourself, and unlock the full potential of your inner voice. With practice and patience, anyone can develop their intuition and learn to live a more intuitive and fulfilling life.

Chapter 5: Enhancing Your Senses

Have you ever experienced a moment where your senses seemed to be heightened? Perhaps you smelled something that triggered a long-forgotten memory or saw a flash of color that seemed to come from nowhere. Our senses are powerful tools that can connect us to our surroundings in profound ways. In fact, they are also connected to our psychic abilities.

In this chapter, we will explore the relationship between our senses and our psychic abilities, and provide techniques for enhancing your senses to develop your psychic potential.

How our senses are connected to psychic abilities

The human body has five primary senses: sight, hearing, taste, smell, and touch. These senses are our connection to the physical world around us. However, many people believe that there is a sixth sense, which is sometimes referred to as extrasensory perception or psychic ability.

Psychic abilities are often associated with our intuition and our ability to tap into a deeper understanding of the world around us. Our senses play a crucial role in this process, as they are the channels through which we receive information.

For example, clairvoyance, which is the ability to see beyond the physical world, is often connected to our sense of sight. Clairaudience, which is the ability to hear beyond the physical world, is connected to our sense of hearing. Similarly, clairsentience, which is the ability to sense beyond the physical world, is connected to our sense of touch and our ability to feel.

By enhancing our senses, we can increase our ability to receive and interpret psychic information. This can help us to develop our psychic abilities and gain a deeper understanding of the world around us.

Techniques for enhancing your senses

Practice mindfulness

Mindfulness is the practice of being present in the moment and paying attention to your surroundings. By practicing mindfulness, you can increase your awareness of your senses and become more attuned to the world around you. Try taking a few minutes each day to focus on your senses. Close your eyes and listen to the sounds around you. Focus on the sensation of your breath moving in and out of your body. Pay attention to the smells in the air and the texture of the surfaces you touch.

Engage in sensory exercises

Engaging in sensory exercises can help to enhance your senses and increase your ability to receive psychic information. Try blindfolding yourself and practicing identifying different smells or textures. Practice listening to music and identifying different instruments or tones. By engaging in these exercises, you can increase your sensitivity to your senses and improve your ability to receive information.

Meditate

Meditation is a powerful tool for developing your psychic abilities and enhancing your senses. By quieting your mind and focusing your attention, you can increase your ability to receive psychic information. Try meditating for a few minutes each day, focusing on your breath or a specific object. As you meditate, pay attention to the sensations in your body and the thoughts and feelings that arise.

Use essential oils

Essential oils are highly concentrated plant extracts that can have powerful effects on the body and mind. Many essential oils have been used for centuries to enhance psychic abilities and increase sensitivity to the senses. Try using essential oils such as lavender, frankincense, or peppermint to enhance your senses and promote relaxation.

Practice visualization

Visualization is a powerful tool for enhancing your senses and developing your psychic abilities. Try visualizing yourself using your senses in different situations. Imagine yourself seeing beyond the physical world, hearing messages from the universe, or feeling the energy of the people around you. By practicing visualization, you can increase your ability to receive psychic information and enhance your overall psychic potential.

Enhancing your senses is a powerful way to develop your psychic abilities and gain a deeper understanding of the world around you . By practicing mindfulness, engaging in sensory exercises, meditating, using essential oils, and practicing visualization, you can increase your sensitivity to your senses and open yourself up to new possibilities.

It's important to note that enhancing your senses and developing your psychic abilities is a journey, and it takes time and practice. Be patient with yourself and don't expect to see results overnight. It's also important to approach these techniques with an open mind and a willingness to explore new possibilities.

In addition to these techniques, it's also important to take care of your physical health. Eating a healthy diet, getting enough sleep, and engaging in regular exercise can all contribute to your overall well-being and enhance your ability to connect with your senses.

It's also important to create a supportive environment for yourself. Surround yourself with people who support your journey and are open to exploring new ideas. Consider joining a meditation or psychic development group to connect with others who are on a similar path.

As you begin to enhance your senses and develop your psychic abilities, you may start to notice subtle changes in your perception of the world around you. You may begin to see colors more vividly, hear sounds more clearly, or feel more attuned to the energy of the people around you. These are all signs that your senses are becoming more finely tuned and that you are opening yourself up to new possibilities.

Enhancing your senses is a powerful way to develop your psychic abilities and gain a deeper understanding of the world around you. By practicing mindfulness, engaging in sensory exercises, meditating, using essential oils, and practicing visualization, you can increase your sensitivity to your senses and open yourself up to new possibilities. Remember to approach these techniques with an open mind and a willingness to explore new ideas, and be patient with yourself as you embark on this journey of self-discovery and growth.

Chapter 6: Opening Your Third Eye

Have you ever heard the term "third eye" and wondered what it means? Or perhaps you have heard that opening your third eye can lead to increased intuition and spiritual insight, but you're not sure where to begin. In this chapter, we will explore the concept of the third eye and provide techniques for opening it to enhance your psychic abilities and deepen your spiritual practice.

What is the third eye?

The third eye, also known as the pineal gland, is a small gland located in the center of the brain. It is shaped like a pinecone, which is where its name comes from. The third eye is considered by many to be the gateway to higher consciousness and spiritual insight.

The third eye is associated with the sixth chakra, also known as the brow chakra. This chakra is located in the center of the forehead and is associated with intuition, insight, and psychic ability. When the third eye is open, it is said to allow us to see beyond the physical world and tap into a deeper understanding of the universe.

Techniques for opening your third eye

Meditation

Meditation is one of the most powerful techniques for opening the third eye. By quieting the mind and focusing your attention, you can increase your awareness of your intuition and spiritual insight. Try meditating for a few minutes each day, focusing your attention on your third eye. Imagine a bright light or a lotus flower opening at the center of your forehead. As you meditate, pay attention to any images, feelings, or messages that arise.

Yoga

Yoga is a physical practice that can also help to open the third eye. Certain poses, such as downward-facing dog and child's pose, can help to stimulate the pineal gland and increase awareness of the third eye. Try incorporating these poses into your yoga practice and focusing your attention on your third eye as you hold the pose.

Visualization

Visualization is a powerful tool for opening the third eye. Try visualizing your third eye as a bright light or a lotus flower opening at the center of your forehead. As you visualize, focus your attention on your intuition and spiritual insight. Imagine yourself tapping into a deeper understanding of the universe and receiving messages from the divine.

Crystal healing

Certain crystals, such as amethyst and clear quartz, are said to be powerful tools for opening the third eye. Try placing a crystal on your forehead or holding it in your hand as you meditate or visualize. As you focus your attention on the crystal, imagine it helping to activate your third eye and increase your awareness of your intuition and spiritual insight.

Sound healing

Sound healing is a powerful tool for opening the third eye. Certain sounds, such as the OM chant or crystal singing bowls, are said to stimulate the pineal gland and increase awareness of the third eye. Try listening to these sounds as you meditate or visualize, focusing your attention on your third eye and allowing the sound to help activate your intuition and spiritual insight.

Aromatherapy

Certain essential oils, such as frankincense and sandalwood, are said to be powerful tools for opening the third eye. Try diffusing these oils in your home or applying them to your third eye as you meditate or visualize. As you focus your attention on the scent, imagine it helping to activate your third eye and increase your awareness of your intuition and spiritual insight.

Opening your third eye can be a powerful tool for enhancing your psychic abilities and deepening your spiritual practice. By incorporating these techniques into your daily routine, you can increase your awareness of your intuition and tap into a deeper understanding of the universe. Remember to be patient with yourself and trust in your own process, as opening your third eye is a unique journey for everyone. It may take time and practice to fully open your third eye, but the benefits can be well worth it.

Benefits of opening your third eye

Opening your third eye can bring many benefits to your life, including:

Increased intuition: As your third eye opens, you may find that your intuition becomes stronger and more accurate. You may be able to sense things that you couldn't before and make decisions based on your gut feelings.

Spiritual insight: Opening your third eye can lead to a deeper understanding of the universe and your place in it. You may gain new insights into your purpose and the meaning of life.

Clarity of thought: As you become more aware of your intuition and spiritual insights, you may find that your thoughts become clearer and more focused. You may be able to see things from a different perspective and make better decisions.

Heightened senses: Some people report that opening their third eye has led to heightened senses, including improved vision and hearing.

Greater creativity: Opening your third eye can also lead to greater creativity and inspiration. You may find that you have new ideas and insights that you can use in your creative pursuits.

Opening your third eye can be a powerful tool for enhancing your psychic abilities and deepening your spiritual practice. By incorporating techniques like meditation, yoga, visualization, crystal healing, sound healing, and aromatherapy into your daily routine, you can increase your awareness of your intuition and tap into a deeper understanding of the universe. Remember to be patient with yourself and trust in your own process, as opening your third eye is a unique journey for everyone. The benefits of opening your third eye can include increased intuition, spiritual insight, clarity of thought, heightened senses, and greater creativity. So why not give it a try and see what insights and experiences you can gain?

Chapter 7: Understanding Symbols

Symbols are all around us, from the logos on our favorite products to the shapes and colors we see in nature. But what exactly are symbols, and why are they important in clairvoyance? In this chapter, we will explore the concept of symbols and provide techniques for interpreting them to enhance your psychic abilities and deepen your spiritual practice.

What are symbols?

A symbol is a representation of an idea or concept, often using an object, image, or word. Symbols are used to communicate complex ideas and emotions in a simple and concise way, allowing us to understand and connect with them on a deeper level. Symbols can be found in many different forms, from the ancient hieroglyphs of Egypt to the modern-day emojis we use in our text messages.

The importance of symbols in clairvoyance

Symbols are a fundamental part of clairvoyance, the ability to see beyond the physical world and tap into a deeper understanding of the universe. When we receive psychic information, it often comes in the form of symbols that represent ideas, emotions, and concepts that are beyond our physical senses.

For example, you may see a butterfly in your mind's eye during a clairvoyant reading. While the butterfly itself is a physical object that you can see with your eyes, the symbol of the butterfly may represent transformation, growth, and the ability to overcome challenges. By understanding the symbolic meaning behind the butterfly, you can gain a deeper understanding of the message being conveyed.

Techniques for interpreting symbols

Journaling

Journaling is a powerful tool for interpreting symbols. Whenever you receive a symbolic message during a psychic reading or in your daily life, write it down in a journal along with any thoughts or emotions that come up for you. As you journal, try to connect with the symbolic meaning behind the message and explore how it relates to your life.

Dream analysis

Dreams are a rich source of symbolic messages, often containing images and themes that represent our deepest thoughts and emotions. If you remember a dream that contains a symbolic message, write it down and explore its meaning using a dream dictionary or by consulting with a psychic or spiritual advisor.

Meditation

Meditation is a powerful tool for connecting with the symbolic messages that come through during clairvoyant readings. Try meditating for a few minutes each day, focusing your attention on a specific symbol that you would like to explore. As you meditate, allow the symbol to reveal its meaning to you, and pay attention to any thoughts, feelings, or emotions that arise.

Tarot and Oracle cards

Tarot and oracle cards are powerful tools for interpreting symbols. Each card contains a unique symbol that represents a specific idea or concept. By using tarot or oracle cards during a clairvoyant reading or in your daily life, you can gain deeper insights into the symbolic messages that are coming through.

Intuition

Perhaps the most important tool for interpreting symbols is your own intuition. Trust your gut instinct and pay attention to any thoughts or emotions that come up for you when you encounter a symbol. Remember that the meaning of a symbol is highly personal and can vary from person to person based on your own experiences and beliefs.

Understanding symbols can be a powerful tool for enhancing your psychic abilities and deepening your spiritual practice. By incorporating these techniques into your daily routine, you can increase your awareness of the symbolic messages that are coming through and gain deeper insights into the universe around you. Remember to be patient with yourself and trust in your own process, as interpreting symbols is a unique and highly personal journey.

Chapter 8: The Chakra System

Have you ever heard of the chakra system and wondered what it is? Or perhaps you are familiar with chakras but not sure how they relate to clairvoyance. In this chapter, we will explore the concept of chakras and their role in clairvoyance. We will also provide techniques for balancing and activating your chakras to enhance your psychic abilities and overall well-being.

What are chakras?

Chakras are centers of energy located throughout the body. The word "chakra" comes from the Sanskrit word for "wheel" or "disk" and refers to the circular shape of these energy centers. There are seven major chakras in the body, each associated with a different area of the body and with specific emotional, mental, and spiritual functions.

The seven major chakras are:

Root chakra (Muladhara): Located at the base of the spine, this chakra is associated with feelings of safety, security, and grounding.

Sacral chakra (Svadhisthana): Located in the lower abdomen, this chakra is associated with creativity, sexuality, and emotions.

Solar plexus chakra (Manipura): Located in the upper abdomen, this chakra is associated with personal power, self-esteem, and confidence.

Heart chakra (Anahata): Located at the center of the chest, this chakra is associated with love, compassion, and connection.

Throat chakra (Vishuddha): Located at the base of the throat, this chakra is associated with communication, self-expression, and creativity.

Third eye chakra (Ajna): Located at the center of the forehead, this chakra is associated with intuition, spiritual insight, and clairvoyance.

Crown chakra (Sahasrara): Located at the top of the head, this chakra is associated with spirituality, enlightenment, and connection to the divine.

The role of chakras in clairvoyance

Chakras play an important role in clairvoyance and other psychic abilities. Each chakra is associated with specific functions related to intuition, insight, and psychic awareness. For example, the third eye chakra, located in the center of the forehead, is associated with clairvoyance and spiritual insight.

When our chakras are balanced and activated, we are more in tune with our intuition and psychic abilities. We are able to tap into a deeper understanding of ourselves and the world around us, and we may experience increased synchronicities and spiritual experiences.

On the other hand, when our chakras are blocked or imbalanced, we may experience physical, emotional, and spiritual symptoms. For example, a blocked third eye chakra may result in difficulty accessing intuition and spiritual insight, while an imbalanced heart chakra may result in feelings of loneliness or disconnection.

Techniques for balancing and activating chakras

There are many techniques for balancing and activating chakras. Here are a few to get you started:

Meditation: Meditation is a powerful tool for balancing and activating chakras. Try meditating for a few minutes each day, focusing your attention on each chakra in turn. As you focus on each chakra, visualize it as a bright, spinning wheel of energy. Imagine the energy flowing freely through the chakra and bringing balance and harmony to your entire system.

Yoga: Yoga is a physical practice that can help to balance and activate chakras. Each yoga pose is associated with specific chakras, and by practicing yoga, you can stimulate and balance each chakra in turn. Try incorporating yoga poses that target each chakra into your practice.

Breathing exercises: Conscious breathing can help to clear and balance the chakras. Sit in a comfortable position and focus on your breath. As you inhale, imagine white light entering your body and flowing through each chakra. As you exhale, imagine any negative energy or blockages leaving your body.

Crystal healing: Crystals are believed to have energetic properties that can help to balance and activate chakras. Different crystals are associated with different chakras, and by placing the appropriate crystal on or near the chakra, you can help to stimulate and balance its energy. For example, amethyst is associated with the third eye chakra, while rose quartz is associated with the heart chakra.

Sound healing: Sound vibrations can also help to balance and activate chakras. You can use singing bowls, tuning forks, or other instruments to produce specific frequencies that resonate with each chakra. As you listen to the sound, imagine it filling and balancing the corresponding chakra.

Chakra meditation: Chakra meditation is a specific type of meditation that focuses on each chakra in turn. Sit in a comfortable position and visualize each chakra as a bright, spinning wheel of energy. Focus on each chakra for several minutes, imagining the energy flowing freely and bringing balance and harmony to your entire system.

The chakra system is an important concept in clairvoyance and other psychic abilities. Each chakra is associated with specific emotional, mental, and spiritual functions, and when our chakras are balanced and activated, we are more in tune with our intuition and psychic abilities. There are many techniques for balancing and activating chakras, including meditation, yoga, breathing exercises, crystal healing, and sound healing. By incorporating these techniques into your daily routine, you can help to balance and activate your chakras, enhance your psychic abilities, and improve your overall well-being.

Chapter 9: The Aura

Have you ever felt someone's energy before you even met them? Or perhaps you've sensed a shift in the atmosphere of a room without any obvious reason. These experiences are often attributed to the aura, an energetic field that surrounds all living things. In this chapter, we will explore the concept of the aura and its importance in clairvoyance. We will also provide techniques for seeing and interpreting the aura.

What is the aura?

The aura is an energy field that surrounds all living things, including humans, animals, and plants. It is made up of subtle energy that is not visible to the naked eye but can be felt and sensed by those who are sensitive to energy. The aura is often described as a luminous field of light that surrounds the body, extending several inches to several feet in all directions.

The aura is composed of multiple layers or levels, each with its own unique frequency and vibration. The seven major layers of the aura are:

The Etheric Body - This layer is closest to the physical body and is associated with physical sensations, such as pain or pleasure.

The Emotional Body - This layer is associated with emotions and feelings, both positive and negative.

The Mental Body - This layer is associated with thoughts and mental activity.

The Astral Body - This layer is associated with dreams, astral projection, and other forms of psychic activity.

The Etheric Template Body - This layer is associated with the blueprint or template for the physical body.

The Celestial Body - This layer is associated with spiritual development and higher consciousness.

The Ketheric Template or Causal Body - This layer is associated with the soul and contains the blueprint for our spiritual path.

The importance of the aura in clairvoyance

The aura plays an important role in clairvoyance and other psychic abilities. When a clairvoyant reader is performing a reading, they are tapping into the energy field of the person they are reading. This includes the person's aura, which can provide valuable information about their physical, emotional, mental, and spiritual state.

The aura can also provide insights into a person's personality traits, strengths, and weaknesses. For example, a person with a strong and vibrant aura may be confident, outgoing, and successful, while a person with a weak and dull aura may be struggling with low energy, depression, or other issues.

By learning to see and interpret the aura, a clairvoyant reader can gain a deeper understanding of their clients and provide more accurate and insightful readings.

Techniques for seeing and interpreting the aura

Seeing and interpreting the aura requires practice and patience. Here are a few techniques to get you started:

Soft Gaze Technique - This technique involves softening your gaze and looking past the physical body to see the aura. To practice this technique, find a person to practice with and have them stand against a plain, light-colored wall. Focus your eyes on the wall behind them, allowing your gaze to soften and relax. You may begin to see a faint outline of their aura, which may appear as a glow or colored haze around their body.

Hand Gaze Technique - This technique involves focusing on the energy field between your hands. To practice this technique, rub your hands together vigorously to generate energy. Then hold your hands about six inches apart, palms facing each other. Focus your attention on the energy field between your hands, allowing yourself to feel the energy. You may begin to see the energy field as a glow or colored haze.

Aura Photography - Aura photography is a popular method for capturing images of the aura. Special cameras are used to capture the energy field surrounding the body, producing images that show the different colors and patterns of the aura. While aura photography can be a fun and interesting way to explore the aura, it is important to remember that the colors and patterns captured in the image may not always accurately reflect a person's true aura.

Sensing the Aura - Another way to practice seeing and interpreting the aura is through sensing the energy field around a person. To do this, stand near a person and allow yourself to become aware of their energy. You may feel a tingling or buzzing sensation, or you may feel a shift in the energy around you. This technique can be helpful in developing your sensitivity to energy and can be a useful tool in clairvoyant readings.

Interpreting the Aura - Once you are able to see or sense the aura, the next step is interpreting what you see. The colors and patterns of the aura can provide valuable information about a person's physical, emotional, mental, and spiritual state. Here are some common aura colors and their meanings:

Red - indicates passion, strength, and energy.

Orange - indicates creativity, ambition, and motivation.

Yellow - indicates intellect, optimism, and confidence.

Green - indicates growth, healing, and balance.

Blue - indicates communication, intuition, and serenity.

Purple - indicates spirituality, intuition, and inner wisdom.

White - indicates purity, clarity, and higher consciousness.

It is important to note that the colors and meanings of the aura can vary depending on the individual and the context in which they are seen. It is also important to approach interpreting the aura with an open mind and to use your intuition and psychic abilities to gain deeper insights into what you are seeing.

The aura is an energy field that surrounds all living things and plays an important role in clairvoyance and other psychic abilities. By learning to see and interpret the aura, you can gain valuable insights into a person's physical, emotional, mental, and spiritual state. With practice and patience, you can develop your ability to see and interpret the aura, adding another tool to your psychic toolkit. Remember to approach the aura with an open mind and to use your intuition and psychic abilities to gain deeper insights into what you are seeing.

Chapter 10: Dreamwork

Have you ever woken up from a dream feeling like it was trying to tell you something important? Or maybe you've had a dream that seemed so vivid and real that it stayed with you long after you woke up. Dreams have been a source of fascination for humans for centuries, and for good reason. Dreams can provide valuable insights into our subconscious mind, our emotions, and even our future. In this chapter, we will explore the importance of dreams in clairvoyance and provide techniques for lucid dreaming and dream interpretation.

The importance of dreams in clairvoyance

Dreams have always been an integral part of clairvoyance and other forms of divination. The ancient Greeks believed that dreams were messages from the gods, while many indigenous cultures believe that dreams are a way to communicate with ancestors or spirit guides. In more modern times, Freud and Jung developed theories about the role of dreams in our psyche, with Freud focusing on the interpretation of symbols and Jung exploring the idea of archetypes.

In clairvoyance, dreams are seen as a way to tap into our intuition and receive messages from the universe. Dreams can provide insights into our deepest fears, desires, and motivations, as well as guidance and warnings about our future. By learning to work with our dreams, we can gain a deeper understanding of ourselves and the world around us.

Techniques for lucid dreaming

Lucid dreaming is a state in which we become aware that we are dreaming while we are still in the dream. This allows us to take control of the dream and consciously direct the experience. Lucid dreaming can be a powerful tool for exploring our subconscious mind and receiving guidance and messages from our intuition.

Here are a few techniques for lucid dreaming:

Reality Checks - Throughout the day, ask yourself whether you are dreaming. Look at your hands, and ask yourself if they look normal. Check your surroundings and see if everything looks as it should. By developing the habit of questioning reality, you are more likely to do the same in your dreams and become aware that you are dreaming.

Mnemonic Induction of Lucid Dreams (MILD) - This technique involves setting an intention to have a lucid dream before going to sleep. Repeat a phrase like "I will have a lucid dream tonight" while visualizing yourself becoming aware that you are dreaming.

Wake-Back-To-Bed (WBTB) - This technique involves waking up after a few hours of sleep, staying awake for 30-60 minutes, and then going back to sleep. This can increase the likelihood of entering a state of lucid dreaming.

Techniques for dream interpretation

Interpreting dreams can be a complex and subjective process, as the symbolism and meaning of dreams can vary widely depending on the individual and their personal experiences. However, there are some general guidelines and techniques that can be helpful in deciphering the messages of our dreams.

Here are a few techniques for dream interpretation:

Journaling - Keep a dream journal by your bedside and record your dreams as soon as you wake up. Write down as much detail as possible, including the emotions you felt, any recurring themes or symbols, and any people or objects that stood out to you. Over time, you may start to see patterns or recurring themes that can provide insights into your subconscious mind.

Free Association - Take a particular symbol or image from your dream and write down everything that comes to mind when you think about it. This can help you uncover hidden meanings and associations that may not be immediately obvious.

Amplification - Amplification involves taking a symbol or image from your dream and exploring its cultural, historical, and mythological associations. For example, if you dreamt of a snake, you could research the symbolism of snakes in different cultures and mythologies to gain a deeper understanding of what the snake may represent in your dream.

Active Imagination - This technique involves entering a meditative state and actively engaging with the symbols and images from your dream. By visualizing the dream scene and interacting with the elements of the dream, you may be able to uncover new insights and gain a deeper understanding of the messages that are being conveyed.

It's important to remember that dream interpretation is not an exact science, and different interpretations may resonate with different individuals. Ultimately, the most important aspect of dreamwork is developing a personal relationship with your dreams and learning to trust your intuition.

Dreams have been a powerful source of guidance and inspiration for humans for centuries. By learning to work with our dreams, we can tap into our intuition, gain insights into our subconscious mind, and receive guidance and warnings about our future. Techniques like lucid dreaming and dream interpretation can be valuable tools in this process, but ultimately the key is to develop a personal relationship with our dreams and learn to trust the messages that they provide. So the next time you wake up from a dream that seems to be trying to tell you something, take a moment to reflect on its message and see where it leads you. Who knows, it could be the key to unlocking your deepest desires and achieving your wildest dreams.

Chapter 11: Automatic Writing

Have you ever felt like there were thoughts or messages inside of you that you couldn't quite access? Maybe you've struggled with writer's block or felt stuck in your creative process. If so, you might be interested in exploring the practice of automatic writing. In this chapter, we will explore what automatic writing is and provide techniques to get started with this powerful tool for accessing your inner wisdom.

What is Automatic Writing?

Automatic writing is a form of writing where the writer allows themselves to write without conscious thought or censorship. In this practice, the writer puts their hand to paper or keyboard and allows the words to flow freely, without judgment or preconceived ideas about what they should be writing. The goal of automatic writing is to access the subconscious mind and receive messages from our intuition, higher self, or spirit guides.

The practice of automatic writing has been used for centuries by spiritual seekers, writers, and artists. Some of the most famous examples of automatic writing come from the work of the Surrealist artists in the early 20th century, who used the technique to create art that reflected the workings of the unconscious mind.

Techniques for Automatic Writing

If you're interested in exploring automatic writing, there are a few techniques that can help you get started. Keep in mind that this practice is highly personal and subjective, so what works for one person may not work for another. The key is to be open and receptive to the messages that come through, without judgment or preconceived ideas about what you "should" be writing.

Here are a few techniques to get started with automatic writing:

Set the Intention

Before you begin, set an intention for your writing session. This could be a question you want to explore, an issue you're struggling with, or simply a desire to connect with your inner wisdom. By setting an intention, you create a focused container for your writing that can help guide the messages that come through.

Get into a Relaxed State

It can be helpful to get into a relaxed state before beginning your automatic writing session. This could involve meditation, deep breathing, or simply taking a few moments to quiet your mind. By calming your mind and body, you create a receptive space for the messages to flow through.

Start Writing

Once you're in a relaxed state, begin writing. Don't worry about grammar, spelling, or punctuation - just let the words flow freely. You may find that the writing starts out slow or disjointed, but as you continue, the messages will become clearer and more coherent.

Keep Writing

The key to automatic writing is to keep writing, even if you feel like you're just repeating yourself or writing nonsense. Trust that the messages will come through, even if they don't make sense at first. By allowing the writing to flow freely, you create a space for your intuition and inner wisdom to speak.

Reflect and Interpret

After your writing session, take some time to reflect on what came through. Look for patterns or recurring themes, and try to interpret the messages that came through. Keep in mind that the interpretation of automatic writing is highly personal and subjective, so trust your own intuition and insights.

Tips for Successful Automatic Writing

Here are a few additional tips to help you make the most of your automatic writing practice:

Practice regularly. Like any skill, automatic writing takes practice. Try to make it a daily or weekly habit to write without conscious thought.

Create a dedicated space. Find a quiet, comfortable space where you can write without distractions. This could be a dedicated writing nook, a cozy corner of your bedroom, or even a spot in nature.

Use a timer. Set a timer for a set amount of time (such as 10 or 15 minutes) to help you stay focused and committed to your writing practice. Knowing that you only have a limited amount of time can also help to alleviate any pressure or anxiety you may feel about the process.

Don't judge or censor your writing. The whole point of automatic writing is to let the words flow freely without any self-censorship or judgment. Don't worry about whether what you're writing is "good" or "bad" - just let it come out.

Be patient. It may take some time before you start to receive clear messages or insights through your automatic writing. Be patient with yourself and the process, and trust that the messages will come through in their own time.

Take care of yourself. Automatic writing can be a powerful tool for self-discovery and personal growth, but it can also be emotionally taxing. Make sure you take care of yourself before and after your writing sessions, and don't be afraid to seek support if you need it.

Automatic writing is a powerful tool for accessing our inner wisdom and intuition. By allowing ourselves to write without conscious thought or censorship, we create a space for messages and insights to flow through from our subconscious mind, higher self, or spirit guides. While the practice of automatic writing is highly personal and subjective, there are techniques and tips that can help us get started and make the most of this powerful tool.

Whether you're a writer, artist, or spiritual seeker, automatic writing can help you tap into your creativity and connect with your inner wisdom. By setting an intention, getting into a relaxed state, and letting the words flow freely, you create a space for insights and messages to come through. With patience, practice, and self-care, automatic writing can become a powerful tool for personal growth, self-discovery, and creative expression.

Chapter 12: Tarot and Oracle Cards

Have you ever been drawn to the mysterious world of tarot and oracle cards? These beautiful and intricate cards have been used for centuries as a tool for divination and self-discovery. In this chapter, we will explore what tarot and oracle cards are and provide techniques for using them in your own spiritual practice.

What are Tarot and Oracle Cards?

Tarot cards are a deck of 78 cards that are typically divided into two categories: the Major Arcana and the Minor Arcana. The Major Arcana consists of 22 cards, each with a specific archetype or theme, such as the Fool, the Magician, and the High Priestess. The Minor Arcana consists of 56 cards, divided into four suits: Cups, Swords, Wands, and Pentacles. Each suit represents a different aspect of life, such as emotions, thoughts, creativity, and material abundance.

Oracle cards, on the other hand, can take many different forms and do not have a standard number of cards. They may feature images, symbols, or words that are intended to offer guidance or insight into a particular question or situation.

Both tarot and oracle cards are used as a tool for divination, or the practice of seeking guidance and insight from a higher power or spiritual realm. They can also be used for self-reflection and personal growth, helping us to explore our own thoughts, emotions, and experiences.

Techniques for Using Tarot and Oracle Cards

If you're interested in using tarot or oracle cards in your spiritual practice, there are a few techniques that can help you get started. Keep in mind that these techniques are highly personal and subjective, so what works for one person may not work for another. The key is to be open and receptive to the messages that come through, without judgment or preconceived ideas about what the cards "should" mean.

Here are a few techniques for using tarot and oracle cards:

Set an Intention

Before you begin your card reading, it can be helpful to set an intention for what you hope to gain from the experience. This could be a question you want to explore, an issue you're struggling with, or simply a desire to connect with your higher self or spirit guides.

Shuffle the Cards

Once you've set your intention, take a moment to shuffle the cards. This can help to clear your mind and create a focused energy for the reading. You may also want to take a few deep breaths or engage in a quick meditation to center yourself before shuffling.

Draw a Card

When you're ready, draw a card from the deck. Take a moment to look at the image or symbol on the card and reflect on what it means to you. Pay attention to any thoughts or feelings that come up, and try to connect them to your intention for the reading.

Interpret the Card

Once you've drawn your card, it's time to interpret its meaning. This can be a highly personal process, and there are many different ways to approach it. Some people prefer to use a guidebook or online resource to help them interpret the card, while others prefer to rely on their own intuition and insights.

Reflect and Take Action

After your reading, take some time to reflect on what you've learned. Look for patterns or recurring themes in the cards you've drawn, and try to apply their insights to your life or situation. Remember that the cards are simply a tool for self-reflection and guidance, and that the real work of personal growth and transformation happens in the actions you take based on the insights you've gained.

Tips for Successful Tarot and Oracle Card Readings

Here are a few additional tips to help you make the most of your tarot and oracle card readings:

Create a sacred space: Before beginning your reading, create a sacred space that feels comfortable and safe for you. This could be a quiet room in your home, a garden, or any other space where you feel relaxed and at peace.

Choose a deck that resonates with you: There are many different tarot and oracle decks available, each with their own unique energy and style. Take some time to explore different decks and choose one that resonates with you on a deep level.

Practice regularly: Like any other spiritual practice, using tarot and oracle cards requires regular practice and dedication. Set aside time each week to work with your cards, and make it a priority in your spiritual practice.

Trust your intuition: When interpreting the cards, it's important to trust your intuition and inner wisdom. The cards may offer guidance or insight, but ultimately, you are the one in control of your life and decisions.

Don't be afraid to ask for help: If you're struggling to interpret a card or understand its meaning, don't be afraid to ask for help. There are many online resources, books, and communities available to support you on your tarot and oracle journey.

Tarot and oracle cards can be a powerful tool for self-reflection, personal growth, and spiritual connection. Whether you're just starting out or have been working with cards for years, there is always something new to discover and explore.

Remember to approach your readings with an open mind and heart, and trust in the messages that come through. With practice and dedication, tarot and oracle cards can become a valuable and transformative part of your spiritual practice.

Chapter 13: Runes and Divination Tools

Have you ever been curious about the ancient practice of using runes and other divination tools for spiritual guidance and self-discovery? In this chapter, we will explore what runes and divination tools are, and provide techniques for using them in your own spiritual practice.

What are Runes and Divination Tools?

Runes are an ancient Germanic alphabet that was used in Scandinavia and other parts of Europe for writing, divination, and magic. The word "rune" comes from the Old Norse word rún, which means "secret" or "mystery."

Each rune has a specific meaning and symbolism, and can be used for divination, meditation, or spellcasting. There are different sets of runes, such as the Elder Futhark, which consists of 24 runes, and the Younger Futhark, which consists of 16 runes.

In addition to runes, there are many other divination tools that can be used for spiritual guidance and self-discovery. These can include tarot and oracle cards, pendulums, crystals, and scrying tools, such as mirrors or bowls of water.

Techniques for Using Runes and Divination Tools

If you're interested in using runes or other divination tools in your spiritual practice, there are a few techniques that can help you get started. As with tarot and oracle cards, these techniques are highly personal and subjective, so what works for one person may not work for another. The key is to be open and receptive to the messages that come through, without judgment or preconceived ideas about what the tools "should" mean.

Here are a few techniques for using runes and divination tools:

Set an Intention

Before you begin your divination practice, it can be helpful to set an intention for what you hope to gain from the experience. This could be a question you want to explore, an issue you're struggling with, or simply a desire to connect with your higher self or spirit guides.

Cleanse and Prepare the Tools

It's important to cleanse and prepare your divination tools before each use. This can help to clear any negative or stagnant energy from the tools and create a focused energy for the divination practice. You can do this by smudging the tools with sage or other cleansing herbs, or by using a crystal or singing bowl to clear the energy.

Choose a Tool

Once you've set your intention and prepared your tools, choose a tool that resonates with you for your divination practice. This could be a rune stone, a tarot card, a crystal, or any other divination tool that you feel drawn to.

Connect with the Tool

Hold the tool in your hand and take a few deep breaths to center yourself. Close your eyes and visualize yourself connecting with the energy of the tool. You may also want to say a quick prayer or affirmation to invite in divine guidance and protection.

Draw a Rune or Choose a Card

When you're ready, draw a rune stone or choose a card from the deck. Take a moment to look at the image or symbol on the rune or card, and reflect on what it means to you. Pay attention to any thoughts or feelings that come up, and try to connect them to your intention for the divination practice.

Interpret the Message

Once you've drawn your rune or card, it's time to interpret its message. This can be a highly personal process, and there are many different ways to approach it. Some people prefer to use a guidebook or online resource to help them interpret the rune or card, while others prefer to rely on their own intuition and insights.

Reflect and Take Action

After your divination practice, take some time to reflect on what you've learned. Look back on the message you received and consider how it relates to your intention or question. You may want to journal about your experience, or simply take a few moments to meditate and integrate the insights you've gained.

It's important to remember that divination tools are not a magical solution to all of life's problems. Rather, they are a tool for self-discovery and spiritual growth. The messages you receive may not always be what you want to hear, but they can be a valuable source of insight and guidance as you navigate your path in life.

In addition to using runes and other divination tools for personal guidance, many people also incorporate them into their spiritual practice for spellcasting or ritual work. For example, runes can be inscribed on candles or talismans to enhance the energy of a spell, or used to create a bindrune for protection or manifestation.

Ultimately, the use of runes and other divination tools is a deeply personal practice that can be tailored to your individual needs and preferences. Whether you use them for daily guidance or special rituals, these tools can be a powerful way to connect with your inner wisdom and intuition.

Runes and divination tools have been used for centuries as a means of spiritual guidance and self-discovery. Whether you're drawn to the ancient symbolism of the runes, the rich imagery of tarot cards, or the energy of crystals and pendulums, there are many different tools available for exploring the mysteries of the universe.

If you're interested in incorporating these tools into your spiritual practice, take some time to explore the different options available and find what resonates with you. Remember to set your intention, cleanse and prepare your tools, and approach the process with an open mind and heart. With time and practice, you may find that these ancient tools become an integral part of your spiritual journey, helping you to connect with your higher self and the divine wisdom that surrounds us all.

Chapter 14: Developing Psychic Protection

Have you ever had the feeling that someone is watching you, or that you are being influenced by negative energy? This may be an indication that you need to develop psychic protection. In this chapter, we will discuss the importance of psychic protection and provide techniques for developing it.

The Importance of Psychic Protection

Psychic protection is a practice of creating a shield of energy around yourself to protect against negative energy and psychic attacks. It is important because we are all energy beings, and our energy fields can be affected by the energy of others. When we are exposed to negative energy, it can affect us in various ways, including physical, emotional, and spiritual.

Psychic protection can also help us to maintain our own energy levels and prevent us from being drained by others. When we are in contact with people who have low energy levels, it can affect our own energy levels and leave us feeling drained and exhausted.

Developing psychic protection can also help us to develop our intuition and psychic abilities. When we are not distracted by negative energy or psychic attacks, we are better able to connect with our inner guidance and receive messages from the spiritual realm.

Techniques for Psychic Protection

There are many different techniques for developing psychic protection, and what works for one person may not work for another. The key is to find a technique that resonates with you and incorporate it into your daily practice.

Here are some techniques for developing psychic protection:

Grounding and Centering

Grounding and centering is a technique for connecting with the earth and your own energy field. To ground yourself, find a quiet place to sit or stand and close your eyes. Visualize roots growing from the bottom of your feet into the earth. Imagine that you are drawing energy up from the earth into your body.

To center yourself, focus your attention on your breath and your energy field. Imagine that you are surrounded by a sphere of white light. Visualize this light expanding and filling your entire body. This technique can help to create a shield of energy around you and protect you from negative energy.

Visualizing a Protective Shield

Visualizing a protective shield is a technique for creating a shield of energy around yourself. To do this, find a quiet place to sit or stand and close your eyes. Visualize a sphere of white light surrounding your body. Imagine that this light is impenetrable and will protect you from negative energy.

You can also imagine a specific color or symbol that represents protection to you. Visualize this color or symbol surrounding you and creating a shield of energy around you.

Crystal Protection

Crystals are powerful tools for psychic protection. They can absorb negative energy and protect you from psychic attacks. To use crystals for protection, choose a crystal that resonates with you and carry it with you throughout the day. You can also place crystals around your home or workplace to create a protective shield.

Some of the best crystals for psychic protection include black tourmaline, black obsidian, and amethyst.

Smudging

Smudging is a technique for clearing negative energy from your energy field and your environment. To smudge, light a bundle of sage or other cleansing herbs and allow the smoke to waft over your body and your surroundings. You can also use a smudge spray or diffuser to achieve the same effect.

This technique can help to clear negative energy and create a protective shield around you.

Setting Boundaries

Setting boundaries is an important aspect of psychic protection. It involves saying "no" to people or situations that do not serve your highest good. When you set clear boundaries, you create a shield of energy around yourself that protects you from negative energy and psychic attacks.

It's important to remember that setting boundaries is not a selfish act. It is an act of self-love and self-care that allows you to maintain your own energy levels and prevent yourself from being drained by others.

Visualization

Visualization is a powerful tool for developing psychic protection. To use visualization, find a quiet place to sit or stand and close your eyes. Visualize a bright white light surrounding your body. Imagine that this light is creating a shield of energy around you that protects you from negative energy.

You can also visualize yourself surrounded by a bubble of light or a cloak of protection. Whatever visualization works for you, focus on it and imagine it becoming stronger and stronger as you practice.

Meditation

Meditation is another powerful tool for developing psychic protection. When you meditate, you quiet your mind and connect with your inner guidance. This allows you to create a shield of energy around yourself and protect yourself from negative energy and psychic attacks.

To meditate, find a quiet place to sit or lie down. Close your eyes and focus on your breath. Imagine that you are surrounded by a sphere of white light that protects you from negative energy. You can also repeat a mantra or affirmation to help you focus your mind and strengthen your shield of protection.

Practice Self-Care

Practicing self-care is an essential aspect of developing psychic protection. When you take care of yourself, you maintain your energy levels and prevent yourself from being drained by others. This can include things like getting enough rest, eating a healthy diet, and engaging in activities that bring you joy.

It's also important to take time for yourself and engage in activities that help you to relax and recharge your batteries. This can include things like taking a bath, going for a walk in nature, or practicing yoga or meditation.

Developing psychic protection is an essential aspect of maintaining your energy levels and protecting yourself from negative energy and psychic attacks. There are many different techniques for developing psychic protection, and what works for one person may not work for another. The key is to find a technique that resonates with you and incorporate it into your daily practice.

Grounding and centering, visualizing a protective shield, using crystals for protection, smudging, setting boundaries, visualization, meditation, and practicing self-care are all powerful techniques for developing psychic protection. By incorporating these techniques into your daily practice, you can create a shield of energy around yourself that protects you from negative energy and psychic attacks and allows you to maintain your own energy levels and connect with your inner guidance.

Chapter 15: Past Lives

Have you ever had a feeling of deja vu or a sense that you've been somewhere before, even though you know you haven't? Perhaps you have dreams or visions that seem to be from another time or place. These experiences could be an indication that you have had past lives, and exploring them can be a powerful tool for developing your clairvoyant abilities. In this chapter, we will discuss the role of past lives in clairvoyance and provide techniques for accessing them.

The Role of Past Lives in Clairvoyance

Past lives are the belief that we have lived multiple lives before our current one. The idea is that our souls are eternal and continue to reincarnate, taking on new bodies and experiences in each lifetime. While not everyone believes in past lives, many people find exploring them to be a helpful tool for understanding their current life and spiritual journey.

For clairvoyants, past lives can play an important role in developing their abilities. It is believed that the experiences and lessons we learned in past lives can carry over into our current one, and exploring those experiences can help us to better understand our gifts and talents.

For example, a clairvoyant who has had past lives as a healer may find that they have a natural ability to sense and heal energy. A clairvoyant who has had past lives as a psychic may find that they have a natural ability to receive messages from the spiritual realm.

Exploring past lives can also help us to heal any unresolved issues or traumas from previous lifetimes. These unresolved issues can manifest as physical or emotional issues in our current life, and exploring the root cause can help us to release them and move forward.

Techniques for Accessing Past Lives

There are many techniques for accessing past lives, and what works for one person may not work for another. The key is to find a technique that resonates with you and approach it with an open mind and heart.

Here are some techniques for accessing past lives:

Meditation

Meditation is a powerful tool for accessing past lives. To do this, find a quiet place to sit or lie down and close your eyes. Take a few deep breaths and allow your body to relax. Once you feel centered, visualize yourself walking down a staircase or path. Imagine that with each step, you are going deeper and deeper into your subconscious mind.

Once you feel fully relaxed and centered, ask yourself to be shown a past life. It may take some time for a vision to come to you, so be patient and allow yourself to be open to whatever comes.

Regression Therapy

Regression therapy is a technique that involves working with a therapist to explore past lives. During a regression therapy session, the therapist will guide you into a deep state of relaxation and lead you through a visualization exercise to access past lives.

Regression therapy can be helpful for those who have difficulty accessing past lives on their own or for those who want to explore their past lives in a more structured environment.

Dreams

Dreams can be a powerful tool for accessing past lives. Before you go to bed, set the intention to explore your past lives in your dreams. You can also use affirmations such as "I am open to receiving messages from my past lives" to help set the stage.

Keep a journal by your bed and write down any dreams or visions you have when you wake up. Over time, you may begin to see patterns or recurring themes that could be indicators of past lives.

Tarot or Oracle Cards

Tarot or oracle cards can be a helpful tool for accessing past lives. Before you begin, set the intention to explore your past lives and ask the cards to show you what you need to know.

Choose a card or spread that resonates with you and allow yourself to be open to the messages that come through. Pay attention to the imagery and symbols on the cards, as they may provide clues to your past lives.

Past Life Regression Audio Recordings

There are many past life regression audio recordings available online that can guide you through a meditation to access past lives. These recordings can be helpful for those who prefer to explore their past lives on their own or who have difficulty visualizing on their own.

When using an audio recording, find a quiet place to listen where you won't be interrupted. Follow the instructions on the recording and allow yourself to fully relax and enter a meditative state. Keep a journal nearby to write down any visions or experiences that come to you.

Exploring past lives can be a powerful tool for clairvoyants to better understand their gifts and talents, as well as to heal any unresolved issues from previous lifetimes. There are many techniques for accessing past lives, and it's important to find one that resonates with you and approach it with an open mind and heart.

Whether you choose to explore your past lives through meditation, regression therapy, dreams, tarot or oracle cards, or audio recordings, the key is to trust the process and be open to whatever comes up. Remember that exploring past lives is a personal journey, and there is no right or wrong way to do it.

By delving into your past lives, you may gain a deeper understanding of yourself and your spiritual journey. You may also gain insights into your current life and the challenges you are facing, allowing you to move forward with greater clarity and purpose. So why not give it a try? You never know what you may discover.

Chapter 16: Connecting with Spirit Guides

Have you ever felt like someone was watching over you, guiding you, or whispering advice in your ear? You may have been connecting with your spirit guides. Spirit guides are non-physical beings that are here to help us on our journey through life. In this chapter, we will discuss who spirit guides are and provide techniques for connecting with them.

Who Are Spirit Guides?

Spirit guides are non-physical beings that act as helpers, protectors, and guides on our spiritual journey. They are often referred to as "guardian angels," but they can take on many forms, including deceased loved ones, animal spirits, or even ascended masters.

Spirit guides are believed to be with us from birth until death and can communicate with us in many different ways, including through signs, symbols, dreams, and intuition. They are here to help us navigate the challenges and opportunities of life and to support us in our spiritual growth.

While everyone has spirit guides, not everyone is aware of them. Some people are more sensitive to their guidance and are able to connect with them more easily, while others may need to develop their intuition and psychic abilities in order to make a connection.

Techniques for Connecting with Spirit Guides

Connecting with your spirit guides can be a powerful tool for gaining insight, clarity, and guidance in your life. Here are some techniques for connecting with your spirit guides:

Meditation

Meditation is a powerful tool for quieting the mind and connecting with spirit guides. To begin, find a quiet place to sit or lie down and close your eyes. Take a few deep breaths and allow your body to relax.

Once you feel centered, imagine yourself surrounded by a protective white light. Ask your spirit guides to come forward and make their presence known to you. You may see images, hear voices, or feel a sense of warmth or comfort.

Allow yourself to receive any messages or guidance that come through. If you have trouble quieting your mind, you can try using guided meditations or binaural beats to help you relax and focus.

Automatic Writing

Automatic writing is a technique that involves allowing your spirit guides to write through you. To begin, find a quiet place to sit and write. Take a few deep breaths and ask your spirit guides to guide your hand.

Begin writing without thinking, allowing the words to flow freely from your hand. Don't worry about grammar or spelling, just allow the words to come through. You may be surprised at what comes out!

Tarot or Oracle Cards

Tarot or oracle cards can be a helpful tool for connecting with your spirit guides. Before you begin, set the intention to connect with your guides and ask them to provide you with guidance through the cards.

Choose a deck that resonates with you and shuffle the cards while focusing on your question or intention. Draw a card and allow the image and message to speak to you. You may also want to journal about your experience and any insights you receive.

Spirit Guide Meditation

This meditation is specifically designed to help you connect with your spirit guides. Find a quiet place to sit or lie down and close your eyes. Take a few deep breaths and allow your body to relax.

Visualize yourself walking through a peaceful forest. Notice the trees, the sound of the birds, and the feeling of the earth beneath your feet. As you walk, imagine a bright light appearing in front of you.

As you get closer, you see that the light is coming from a being of pure love and light. This is your spirit guide. Take a moment to connect with them, feeling their energy and love.

Ask your spirit guide to show you a sign or symbol that you can use to connect with them in the future. This could be a color, an image, or a word. Thank your spirit guide for their presence and guidance, and when you're ready, slowly return to the present moment.

Intuitive Writing

Intuitive writing is another technique that can help you connect with your spirit guides. To begin, find a quiet place to sit and write. Take a few deep breaths and ask your spirit guides to guide your hand.

Begin writing with a specific question or intention in mind. Allow the words to flow freely, without judgment or editing. You may find that your writing takes on a different tone or style than your usual writing, or that new ideas and insights come through.

As you finish your writing, take a moment to thank your spirit guides for their guidance and support.

Connecting with your spirit guides can be a powerful tool for gaining insight, clarity, and guidance in your life. Remember that spirit guides are here to help and support you, so don't be afraid to ask for their guidance and trust the messages that come through.

Whether you choose to use meditation, automatic writing, tarot or oracle cards, or intuitive writing, find a technique that resonates with you and practice it regularly. The more you connect with your spirit guides, the stronger your connection will become.

As with any spiritual practice, it's important to approach connecting with your spirit guides with an open mind and heart. Trust that your guides have your highest good in mind and are here to support you on your journey. With practice and patience, you can develop a deep and meaningful connection with your spirit guides.

Chapter 17: Mediumship

Have you ever wondered if it's possible to communicate with loved ones who have passed away? Or have you ever had a strong feeling that someone who has crossed over is trying to reach you? If so, you may be interested in learning about mediumship. In this chapter, we will discuss what mediumship is and provide techniques for communicating with the spirit world.

What is Mediumship?

Mediumship is the practice of communicating with spirits of the deceased. A medium is someone who acts as a channel between the physical world and the spirit world, relaying messages from loved ones who have passed away to those still living. Mediumship is based on the belief that consciousness continues after death and that spirits can communicate with the living.

There are two main types of mediumship: mental mediumship and physical mediumship. Mental mediumship involves the medium receiving messages from spirits through their thoughts, feelings, and intuition. Physical mediumship involves more tangible forms of communication, such as objects moving, voices speaking, or physical touch.

Mediumship can be a deeply emotional and transformative experience for both the medium and the person receiving the message. It can provide comfort, closure, and healing to those who are grieving and can offer insight and guidance for those seeking spiritual growth.

Techniques for Communicating with the Spirit World

If you are interested in communicating with the spirit world, there are a number of techniques you can try. Here are some of the most common:

Meditation

Meditation is a powerful tool for quieting the mind and opening yourself up to the spirit world. To begin, find a quiet place to sit or lie down and close your eyes. Take a few deep breaths and allow your body to relax.

Once you feel centered, imagine yourself surrounded by a protective white light. Ask for the presence of your loved ones in spirit or your spirit guides. You may see images, hear voices, or feel a sense of warmth or comfort.

Allow yourself to receive any messages or guidance that come through. If you have trouble quieting your mind, you can try using guided meditations or binaural beats to help you relax and focus.

Automatic Writing

Automatic writing is a technique that involves allowing spirits to write through you. To begin, find a quiet place to sit and write. Take a few deep breaths and ask for the presence of your loved ones in spirit or your spirit guides.

Begin writing without thinking, allowing the words to flow freely from your hand. Don't worry about grammar or spelling, just allow the words to come through. You may be surprised at what comes out!

Clairvoyance

Clairvoyance is the ability to receive information through psychic visions. To begin, find a quiet place to sit or lie down and close your eyes. Take a few deep breaths and allow your body to relax.

Once you feel centered, ask for the presence of your loved ones in spirit or your spirit guides. Allow any images, colors, or symbols to come through. These may be symbolic of a message that your loved one is trying to convey.

It's important to note that clairvoyant messages can be subtle and may require interpretation. Trust in the information that you receive and allow yourself to be open to whatever comes through.

Mediumship Circles

A mediumship circle is a group of people who come together to communicate with spirits. It is led by a medium who acts as a channel for the spirits to communicate through. The circle provides a supportive and safe environment for participants to connect with their loved ones in spirit.

In a mediumship circle, the medium may use a variety of techniques to communicate with the spirits, including automatic writing, clairvoyance, and clairaudience. Participants may also have the opportunity to receive messages from their loved ones through the medium.

If you are interested in joining a mediumship circle, look for local groups or classes in your area. You can also find online circles that meet virtually.

Physical Mediumship

Physical mediumship involves more tangible forms of communication with the spirit world, such as objects moving, voices speaking, or physical touch. This type of mediumship is less common and often requires more advanced skills and training.

Physical mediumship can take many forms, including table tipping, séances, and materialization. In table tipping, participants place their hands on a table and ask spirits to move it in response to their questions. In a séance, participants sit in a circle and the medium acts as a channel for the spirits to communicate through. Materialization involves the physical manifestation of a spirit in the room.

It's important to note that physical mediumship can be unpredictable and can sometimes be frightening for participants. It's important to work with experienced mediums and to ensure that the environment is safe and supportive.

Tips for Developing Mediumship Skills

Developing mediumship skills takes time and practice. Here are some tips for improving your abilities:

Practice meditation regularly to quiet your mind and open yourself up to the spirit world.

Keep a journal to record any messages or experiences you have during your mediumship practice.

Work with a mentor or experienced medium to receive guidance and support.

Trust in the messages and images that come through, even if they don't always make sense at first.

Focus on developing your intuition and learning to trust your instincts.

Stay grounded and centered by connecting with nature, practicing self-care, and surrounding yourself with supportive people.

Mediumship can be a powerful tool for connecting with loved ones who have passed away and for receiving guidance and insight from the spirit world. Whether you are just beginning your journey or are an experienced medium, there are a variety of techniques you can use to deepen your connection with the spirit world. Remember to stay open, stay grounded, and trust in the messages that come through. With practice and patience, you can develop your mediumship skills and experience the transformative power of spirit communication.

Chapter 18: Psychic Healing

Have you ever heard of psychic healing? It's a powerful tool that can help heal not just the physical body, but the mind and spirit as well. In this chapter, we'll explore the role of psychic healing in clairvoyance and provide techniques for psychic healing.

The Role of Psychic Healing in Clairvoyance

Psychic healing is the practice of using the power of the mind to promote healing in the body. It is based on the idea that the body and mind are connected and that thoughts and emotions can affect physical health. Psychic healing can be used to heal physical ailments, emotional wounds, and even spiritual imbalances.

In the context of clairvoyance, psychic healing is often used to help clients heal past traumas, release negative emotions, and promote overall wellness. When a clairvoyant is able to tap into their psychic abilities to facilitate healing, it can be a powerful and transformative experience for both the clairvoyant and the client.

Psychic healing can be used in conjunction with other healing modalities, such as energy healing or traditional medicine. It can also be used as a standalone practice for those seeking a more holistic approach to healing.

Techniques for Psychic Healing

There are a variety of techniques that can be used for psychic healing. Here are some of the most common:

Visualization

Visualization is a powerful tool for promoting healing. To begin, find a quiet place to sit or lie down and close your eyes. Take a few deep breaths and allow your body to relax.

Once you feel centered, begin to visualize yourself surrounded by a healing light. You may imagine this light as a particular color or simply as a bright, glowing energy. Allow the light to fill your entire body, penetrating every cell and tissue.

As you visualize this healing light, you may also want to focus on a particular area of your body that needs healing. Imagine the light flowing directly to that area, bringing healing and restoration.

Affirmations

Affirmations are positive statements that can help shift your mindset and promote healing. To use affirmations for psychic healing, begin by identifying a specific area of your life or health that you want to improve.

For example, if you are struggling with anxiety, you might use affirmations such as "I am calm and at peace" or "I trust in the universe to guide me." Repeat these affirmations to yourself throughout the day, focusing on the positive outcomes you hope to achieve.

Crystals

Crystals have long been used for their healing properties. To use crystals for psychic healing, you can either hold them in your hand or place them on or near the area of your body that needs healing.

Some popular healing crystals include:

Amethyst: for promoting relaxation and reducing stress

Clear quartz: for amplifying energy and promoting clarity

Rose quartz: for promoting love and emotional healing

Citrine: for promoting abundance and success

Sound Healing

Sound healing involves using sound vibrations to promote healing. This can be done through various methods, such as chanting, singing bowls, or tuning forks.

To use sound healing for psychic healing, you may want to find a quiet place to sit or lie down and allow yourself to be surrounded by the sound. You may also want to focus on a particular area of your body that needs healing, allowing the sound vibrations to penetrate deeply.

It's important to note that while these techniques can be powerful tools for promoting healing, they should not be used as a substitute for professional medical care. If you are experiencing serious physical or mental health issues, it's important to seek the guidance of a qualified medical professional.

Psychic healing can be a powerful tool for promoting healing in the body, mind, and spirit. By tapping into your psychic abilities and using techniques such as visualization, affirmations, crystals, and sound healing, you can promote overall wellness and heal past traumas and emotional wounds.

In the context of clairvoyance, psychic healing can be a transformative experience for both the clairvoyant and the client. By using their psychic abilities to facilitate healing, a clairvoyant can help their clients release negative emotions, promote emotional healing, and ultimately achieve a greater sense of peace and well-being.

It's important to remember that while psychic healing can be a powerful tool, it should not be used as a substitute for professional medical care. If you are experiencing serious physical or mental health issues, it's important to seek the guidance of a qualified medical professional.

Overall, psychic healing offers a holistic approach to healing that can complement traditional medical treatments. By using the power of the mind to promote healing, we can tap into our own innate healing abilities and achieve a greater sense of well-being and balance in our lives.

Chapter 19: Energy Healing

Have you ever felt like you needed a boost of energy or that your body was out of balance? Energy healing is a practice that can help restore balance and promote healing in the body. In this chapter, we'll explore the role of energy healing in clairvoyance and provide techniques for energy healing.

The Role of Energy Healing in Clairvoyance

Energy healing is based on the idea that the body is made up of energy fields and that disruptions or imbalances in these fields can lead to physical, emotional, or spiritual illness. Energy healers work to restore balance in the body's energy fields, promoting healing and overall well-being.

In the context of clairvoyance, energy healing can be used to help clients release negative energy, heal past traumas, and promote overall balance and wellness. When a clairvoyant is able to tap into their psychic abilities to facilitate energy healing, it can be a powerful and transformative experience for both the clairvoyant and the client.

Energy healing can be used in conjunction with other healing modalities, such as traditional medicine or psychic healing. It can also be used as a standalone practice for those seeking a more holistic approach to healing.

Techniques for Energy Healing

There are a variety of techniques that can be used for energy healing. Here are some of the most common:

Reiki

Reiki is a popular form of energy healing that involves the use of hands-on or hands-off techniques to promote healing. The practitioner uses their hands to channel energy into the client's body, promoting relaxation, balance, and overall wellness.

To receive Reiki, a client will typically lie down on a massage table while the practitioner places their hands on or near the client's body. The practitioner will use a variety of hand positions, working to balance the client's energy fields and promote healing.

Chakra Balancing

Chakras are energy centers located throughout the body that are believed to be connected to different aspects of physical, emotional, and spiritual health. When chakras are out of balance, it can lead to illness or discomfort.

Chakra balancing is a technique that involves working to restore balance in the body's chakras. This can be done through a variety of methods, such as meditation, visualization, or the use of crystals.

To balance your chakras, you may want to begin by identifying which chakras are out of balance. Each chakra is associated with a different color, so you may want to focus on visualizing that color as you work to restore balance.

Once you've identified which chakras need balancing, you can use a variety of techniques to promote healing. For example, you may want to visualize a spinning wheel of light at each chakra, working to clear any blockages and restore balance.

Crystal Healing

Crystals have long been used for their healing properties. Each crystal is believed to have a unique energy that can help promote healing and balance in the body.

To use crystals for energy healing, you can either hold them in your hand or place them on or near the area of your body that needs healing. Some popular healing crystals include:

Amethyst: for promoting relaxation and reducing stress

Clear quartz: for amplifying energy and promoting clarity

Rose quartz: for promoting love and emotional healing

Citrine: for promoting abundance and success

Sound Healing

Sound healing involves using sound vibrations to promote healing. This can be done through various methods, such as chanting, singing bowls, or tuning forks.

To use sound healing for energy healing, you may want to find a quiet place to sit or lie down and allow yourself to be surrounded by the sound. You may also want to focus on a particular area of your body that needs healing, allowing the sound vibrations to penetrate deeply.

As you explore different energy healing techniques, it's important to remember that each person's experience with energy healing will be unique. What works for one person may not work for another, and it's important to find the technique that resonates with you.

In addition to these techniques, there are also many other forms of energy healing that you may want to explore. Some people may find that acupuncture, massage therapy, or yoga can be helpful in promoting balance and healing in the body.

It's also important to note that energy healing should not be used as a substitute for medical treatment. While energy healing can be a powerful tool for promoting wellness, it's important to seek medical attention for any serious health concerns.

Energy healing is a powerful practice that can help promote balance and healing in the body. In the context of clairvoyance, energy healing can be used to help clients release negative energy, heal past traumas, and promote overall wellness.

There are a variety of techniques that can be used for energy healing, including Reiki, chakra balancing, crystal healing, and sound healing. Each technique offers its own unique benefits, and it's important to find the technique that resonates with you.

As you explore energy healing, remember that it's not a substitute for medical treatment. If you have any serious health concerns, it's important to seek medical attention.

With practice and dedication, energy healing can be a powerful tool for promoting healing and wellness in the body. Whether you're seeking to heal past traumas or simply promote overall balance and wellness, energy healing can be a transformative practice that can help you achieve your goals.

Chapter 20: Numerology

Have you ever noticed that certain numbers seem to show up in your life over and over again? Maybe you always look at the clock at exactly 11:11 or you notice that your address or phone number contains repeating digits. Numerology is the study of the symbolism and meaning behind numbers and how they can be used to gain insight into our lives. In this chapter, we'll explore what numerology is and provide techniques for using numerology.

What is Numerology?

Numerology is the study of numbers and their symbolism. It is based on the belief that numbers have a vibrational frequency and that this frequency can be used to gain insight into our lives and personalities.

In numerology, each number is associated with certain characteristics and energies. These characteristics can be used to gain insight into our own personalities, as well as the personalities of others. Numerology can also be used to gain insight into the events and circumstances in our lives.

There are several different types of numerology, including Chaldean numerology, Pythagorean numerology, and Kabbalistic numerology. Each of these approaches has its own unique methodology and interpretation of numbers.

Techniques for Using Numerology

There are many techniques for using numerology to gain insight into our lives. Here are some of the most common:

Life Path Number

The life path number is one of the most important numbers in numerology. It is calculated based on your date of birth and represents the path you are destined to take in life.

To calculate your life path number, you need to add up the digits of your date of birth. For example, if you were born on July 4, 1985, you would add $7 + 4 + 1 + 9 + 8 + 5 = 34$. You would then add the digits of 34 together $(3 + 4 = 7)$, giving you a life path number of 7.

Each life path number is associated with certain characteristics and energies. For example, those with a life path number of 1 are said to be independent, ambitious, and confident, while those with a life path number of 9 are said to be compassionate, creative, and humanitarian.

Numerology Chart

A numerology chart is a tool that can be used to gain insight into the various numbers that are associated with your life. It can help you understand the energies and characteristics that are associated with each number, as well as how these energies are playing out in your life.

To create a numerology chart, you will need to calculate your life path number, as well as your expression number and your soul urge number. Your expression number represents your talents and abilities, while your soul urge number represents your inner desires and motivations.

Each number on the numerology chart is associated with specific characteristics and energies. By studying your numerology chart, you can gain insight into your strengths and weaknesses, as well as the events and circumstances that are likely to occur in your life.

Name Analysis

In numerology, each letter of the alphabet is associated with a specific number. By adding up the numbers associated with the letters in your name, you can gain insight into your personality and the energies that are associated with your name.

To perform a name analysis, you will need to assign a number to each letter of your name based on a numerology chart. You will then add up the numbers associated with each letter to arrive at a single digit number.

Each number is associated with certain energies and characteristics. By studying the number associated with your name, you can gain insight into your strengths and weaknesses, as well as the events and circumstances that are likely to occur in your life.

Numerology is a fascinating tool for gaining insight into our lives and personalities. By studying the symbolism and meaning behind numbers, we can gain a deeper understanding of ourselves and the world around us. Whether you are new to numerology or have been studying it for years, there are many techniques that you can use to gain insight and clarity.

One important thing to keep in mind when using numerology is that it is not a substitute for personal responsibility and free will. Numerology can provide guidance and insight, but ultimately it is up to us to make our own choices and take responsibility for our lives.

If you are interested in exploring numerology further, there are many resources available online and in books. Keep an open mind and be willing to experiment with different techniques to see what works best for you. With practice and patience, numerology can become a powerful tool for self-discovery and personal growth.

Chapter 21: Astrology

Have you ever wondered why you feel more energized and enthusiastic during certain times of the year? Or why you seem to have a natural affinity with certain people? Astrology may hold the answers you're looking for. Astrology is the study of the movements and relative positions of celestial bodies, such as planets and stars, and their influence on human affairs and natural world. In this chapter, we will explore what astrology is and provide techniques for using astrology to gain insight into our lives.

What is Astrology?

Astrology is an ancient practice that has been used for thousands of years to gain insight into human affairs and the natural world. Astrology is based on the belief that there is a relationship between the movements and positions of celestial bodies and events that occur on earth.

In astrology, the position of the sun, moon, and planets at the time of a person's birth are thought to have a significant influence on their personality and life path. Astrology also takes into account the relationship between the planets and stars at any given time, as these can indicate the energetic climate and potential opportunities and challenges that individuals may face.

There are many different types of astrology, including Western astrology, Vedic astrology, and Chinese astrology. Each of these systems has its own unique methodology and interpretation of the celestial bodies and their influence on human affairs.

Techniques for Using Astrology

There are many techniques for using astrology to gain insight into our lives. Here are some of the most common:

Natal Chart Analysis

A natal chart is a tool that can be used to gain insight into the astrological influences at the time of a person's birth. It is also known as a birth chart.

To create a natal chart, you need to know the date, time, and location of your birth. The natal chart will show the positions of the sun, moon, and planets at the time of your birth.

Each planet is associated with certain energies and characteristics. By studying your natal chart, you can gain insight into your personality, strengths, weaknesses, and life path. It can also reveal potential opportunities and challenges that you may face throughout your life.

Transit Analysis

A transit analysis is a tool that can be used to gain insight into the astrological influences at any given time. It looks at the positions of the planets in relation to your natal chart.

By studying the transits, you can gain insight into the energetic climate and potential opportunities and challenges that you may face. This can help you make decisions and take action in alignment with the energies at play.

Compatibility Analysis

Compatibility analysis is a tool that can be used to gain insight into the potential dynamics between two individuals. It is based on the position of the planets at the time of each person's birth and how they interact with one another.

By studying the compatibility between two individuals, you can gain insight into the strengths and challenges of the relationship. This can help you navigate the relationship in a way that is in alignment with both individuals' needs and desires.

Astrological Forecasting

Astrological forecasting is a tool that can be used to gain insight into the potential opportunities and challenges that may arise over a certain period. It looks at the positions of the planets and stars at a given time and how they may impact individuals and events on earth.

By studying the astrological forecast, you can gain insight into the energetic climate and potential opportunities and challenges that may arise. This can help you make decisions and take action in alignment with the energies at play.

Astrology is a fascinating tool for gaining insight into our lives and the world around us. By studying the movements and positions of celestial bodies, we can gain insight into our personalities, strengths, weaknesses, and life paths. We can also gain insight into the potential opportunities and challenges that we may face, as well as the energetic climate at any given time.

While astrology is not a science and should not be relied upon as the sole source of guidance in our lives, it can be a valuable tool for gaining insight and understanding. It can help us navigate our relationships, make decisions, and take action in alignment with the energies at play.

Whether you're a seasoned astrology enthusiast or just curious to learn more, there are many resources available to help you explore this fascinating field. Books, online resources, and professional astrologers can all provide valuable information and guidance on how to use astrology to gain insight into your life and the world around you.

Remember, astrology is not about predicting the future or finding quick fixes to our problems. It is about gaining a deeper understanding of ourselves and the world around us, and using that knowledge to make decisions and take action in alignment with our highest selves.

So, if you're curious about astrology, don't be afraid to dive in and explore. Who knows, you may just discover a new way of understanding and navigating your life that you never knew existed.

Chapter 22: Crystals and Gemstones

Have you ever been drawn to the beauty of a sparkling gemstone or crystal? Perhaps you've felt a sense of calm and relaxation when holding a smooth, polished stone. Crystals and gemstones have been used for centuries in spiritual and healing practices, and their use continues to grow in popularity today. In this chapter, we will explore what crystals and gemstones are and provide techniques for using them to enhance your life.

What are Crystals and Gemstones?

Crystals and gemstones are naturally occurring minerals that have been used for their beauty, healing properties, and spiritual significance for thousands of years. These stones come in a variety of shapes, sizes, and colors, and are often prized for their unique patterns and properties.

Each crystal and gemstone has its own unique energy and vibration, and is believed to have certain healing and metaphysical properties. Some stones are said to promote physical healing, while others are thought to enhance emotional and spiritual well-being.

Techniques for Using Crystals and Gemstones

There are many different techniques for using crystals and gemstones to enhance your life. Here are some of the most common:

Crystal Healing

Crystal healing is a practice that uses the energy and vibration of crystals to promote physical, emotional, and spiritual healing. This practice is based on the belief that each crystal and gemstone has its own unique energy and healing properties.

To use crystals for healing, you can place them on or near the body, or carry them with you throughout the day. Each stone is believed to have a specific healing property, so it's important to choose the right stone for your needs.

Meditation

Meditation is a powerful practice for quieting the mind and reducing stress and anxiety. Many people find that using crystals and gemstones during meditation can enhance the practice and deepen the experience.

To use crystals and gemstones during meditation, simply hold the stone in your hand or place it in front of you. Focus on the energy and vibration of the stone, and allow it to guide you into a deeper state of relaxation and awareness.

Crystal Grids

Crystal grids are a powerful way to amplify the energy of crystals and gemstones. A crystal grid is a pattern of stones that are arranged in a specific way to create a specific energy field.

To create a crystal grid, you will need a selection of stones and a specific intention or goal in mind. You can arrange the stones in a pattern that resonates with your intention, and then activate the grid by visualizing the energy flowing between the stones.

Wearing Crystals

Wearing crystals and gemstones is a popular way to benefit from their energy and vibration throughout the day. You can wear crystals as jewelry, or carry them with you in a pouch or pocket.

Each crystal has its own unique properties, so it's important to choose a stone that aligns with your needs and goals. For example, amethyst is a stone that is often used for spiritual growth and intuition, while rose quartz is associated with love and emotional healing.

Using Crystals in Your Home

Using crystals and gemstones in your home can create a peaceful and harmonious environment. You can place crystals throughout your home to enhance the energy of each room, or create a crystal altar to focus your intentions and goals.

To use crystals in your home, choose stones that align with your intention and place them in a location that feels right to you. For example, you may choose to place a piece of citrine in your abundance corner to attract prosperity and success.

Crystals and gemstones are powerful tools for enhancing your life and promoting healing and well-being. By working with these stones, you can tap into their unique energy and vibration to align with your intentions and goals. Whether you use crystals for healing, meditation , or simply to add beauty to your surroundings, there are many ways to incorporate these precious minerals into your life.

It's important to note that while crystals and gemstones can be incredibly beneficial, they should never replace medical treatment or professional therapy. If you have a medical condition or mental health concern, it's important to seek the advice of a qualified healthcare professional.

In addition, it's important to choose high-quality crystals and gemstones from a reputable source. Many crystals on the market are treated or synthetic, which can diminish their energy and healing properties. When purchasing crystals, look for a seller that is transparent about their sourcing and provides information on the quality and authenticity of their stones.

Working with crystals and gemstones can be a transformative experience that helps you tap into your own inner wisdom and strength. Whether you're drawn to the beauty of these stones or the potential for healing and growth, there are endless ways to incorporate them into your daily life. So go ahead, explore the world of crystals and gemstones, and discover the magic they hold within.

Chapter 23: Feng Shui

Have you ever walked into a room and immediately felt a sense of calm and balance? Or, perhaps you've entered a space and felt uncomfortable or uneasy, even though you couldn't quite put your finger on why. These feelings are often attributed to the principles of feng shui, an ancient Chinese art and science of creating balance and harmony in living spaces. In this chapter, we will explore what feng shui is and provide techniques for using it to enhance your home and life.

What is Feng Shui?

Feng shui is an ancient Chinese art and science of creating balance and harmony in living spaces. The principles of feng shui are based on the concept of qi, or life force energy, which is believed to flow through all things in the universe, including the spaces we inhabit. The goal of feng shui is to create a harmonious and balanced environment that supports the flow of qi, promoting health, happiness, and prosperity.

The principles of feng shui can be applied to any living space, from a small apartment to a large office building. By creating a harmonious environment, you can promote positive energy flow and support your goals and intentions.

Techniques for Using Feng Shui

There are many different techniques for using feng shui to enhance your home and life. Here are some of the most common:

Clear the Clutter

One of the most important principles of feng shui is to clear the clutter from your living space. Clutter can block the flow of qi, creating stagnant energy that can contribute to stress and negativity. By clearing the clutter from your home, you can create a sense of spaciousness and allow the flow of positive energy.

Start by going through each room in your home and identifying items that you no longer need or use. Donate or sell these items, or discard them if they are no longer useful. You may also want to consider organizing your belongings in a way that is aesthetically pleasing and promotes positive energy flow.

Use Color

Color plays an important role in feng shui, as each color is believed to have a unique energy and vibration. By using color strategically in your home, you can create a sense of balance and harmony.

Choose colors that align with your intentions and goals. For example, if you want to promote relaxation and calm in your bedroom, you may want to use soft blues or greens. If you want to promote creativity and inspiration in your home office, you may want to use bright, bold colors like red or orange.

Maximize Natural Light

Natural light is a powerful tool in feng shui, as it promotes positive energy flow and helps to create a sense of spaciousness and openness. Maximize natural light in your home by using light and airy window treatments, keeping windows clean and free of obstructions, and using mirrors to reflect light.

If you have areas in your home that are dark or receive little natural light, consider using artificial lighting to create a sense of balance and harmony.

Use Mirrors

Mirrors are another powerful tool in feng shui, as they can be used to reflect light and create a sense of spaciousness and openness. Mirrors can also be used to reflect positive energy and deflect negative energy.

When using mirrors in your home, be mindful of their placement. Avoid placing mirrors directly across from each other, as this can create a sense of chaos and confusion. Instead, place mirrors strategically to reflect positive energy and create a sense of balance and harmony.

Incorporate Nature

Incorporating elements of nature into your home is a key principle of feng shui, as nature is believed to promote positive energy flow and support well-being. You can incorporate nature into your home in a variety of ways, such as adding plants, using natural materials like wood and stone, and incorporating water features.

Plants are a particularly powerful way to incorporate nature into your home. They not only add visual appeal, but also help to purify the air and promote a sense of calm and tranquility. Choose plants that thrive in the lighting and climate conditions of your home, and place them in areas where you want to promote positive energy flow.

When incorporating water features into your home, be mindful of their placement. Water is a powerful symbol of abundance and prosperity, but it can also represent the unknown and unpredictable. Avoid placing water features in areas that are associated with negative energy or conflict, and be sure to keep them clean and well-maintained.

Arrange Furniture Thoughtfully

The way you arrange your furniture can have a significant impact on the flow of energy in your home. Arrange furniture in a way that promotes balance and harmony, and be mindful of the function of each room.

In the bedroom, for example, it is important to place the bed in a position where you can see the door, but not directly in line with it. This creates a sense of safety and security while you sleep. In the living room, arrange furniture in a way that encourages conversation and socializing, such as grouping chairs and sofas together.

Be mindful of the function of each room when arranging furniture. For example, if you have a home office, arrange the desk in a way that promotes productivity and focus.

Feng shui is a powerful tool for creating balance and harmony in your living spaces. By incorporating these techniques into your home, you can promote positive energy flow, support your goals and intentions, and enhance your overall well-being.

Remember to start by clearing the clutter from your home, and use color, natural light, mirrors, and elements of nature strategically to create a sense of balance and harmony. Arrange furniture thoughtfully to promote positive energy flow, and be mindful of the function of each room.

With these techniques, you can transform your living spaces into environments that support your health, happiness, and prosperity. So, go ahead and give feng shui a try – you may be surprised at the positive changes it brings to your life.

Chapter 24: Remote Viewing

Have you ever had a hunch about something that turned out to be true? Or perhaps you've had a vivid dream that seemed too real to be just a product of your imagination. These experiences might actually be a form of remote viewing, a practice that allows individuals to access information about people, places, or events that are not within their physical presence. In this chapter, we will explore what remote viewing is, its history, and techniques for practicing it.

What is Remote Viewing?

Remote viewing is a psychic practice that allows individuals to perceive information about people, places, or events that are beyond their physical location. This information is often obtained through a form of extrasensory perception (ESP), such as clairvoyance (the ability to see beyond what is visible to the naked eye) or telepathy (the ability to receive information from someone else's mind).

Remote viewing has been studied extensively by the U.S. government and military as a tool for intelligence gathering. In the 1970s and 1980s, a program called Stargate was created to investigate the potential of remote viewing for military purposes. The program was eventually disbanded, but the findings of the research have been a topic of ongoing interest and controversy.

Techniques for Remote Viewing

Remote viewing can be practiced by anyone, regardless of their level of psychic ability. Here are some techniques for practicing remote viewing:

Relaxation

One of the most important aspects of remote viewing is relaxation. To begin, find a quiet and comfortable place where you can sit or lie down without being disturbed. Take deep breaths and focus on releasing any tension or stress in your body. Allow yourself to become fully present in the moment.

Visualization

Visualization is an important part of remote viewing, as it helps to focus the mind and access the subconscious. Begin by imagining a blank canvas in your mind's eye. Visualize yourself standing in front of this canvas, holding a paintbrush. With each stroke of the brush, allow an image to emerge on the canvas. The image might be abstract or concrete, and it might not make sense at first. Trust your intuition and allow the image to unfold.

Target Practice

To practice remote viewing, it's helpful to have a target to focus on. This can be any object or location that you don't have access to physically. Start by writing down a target on a piece of paper, such as a picture of a landmark or a description of an object. Hold the paper in your hand and focus on the target. Allow yourself to become fully immersed in the image of the target in your mind's eye. Take note of any impressions or sensations that come to you.

Partner Practice

Remote viewing can also be practiced with a partner. Choose someone you trust and feel comfortable with, and have them choose a target for you to focus on. They can write down the target on a piece of paper and hold it in their hand, without showing it to you. Focus on the image of the target in your mind's eye and describe what you see, hear, or feel. Your partner can then reveal the target to you and you can compare your impressions with the actual target.

Dream Practice

Dreams can be a powerful tool for remote viewing, as they allow us to access our subconscious mind. Before going to bed, focus on a target and ask your subconscious to provide you with information about the target in your dreams. Keep a journal by your bed to record any impressions or sensations you experience in your dreams. Compare these with the actual target to see how accurate your impressions were.

Remote viewing is a practice that allows individuals to access information about people, places, or events that are beyond their physical location. While it has been studied extensively by the U.S. government and military for intelligence gathering, remote viewing can also be practiced by anyone interested in exploring their own psychic abilities. Techniques such as relaxation, visualization, target practice, partner practice, and dream practice can all be used to enhance one's remote viewing abilities.

It's important to note that remote viewing is not a guarantee of accuracy, and it should not be relied upon as a substitute for traditional forms of research or investigation. However, for those interested in exploring the limits of their own consciousness, remote viewing can be a fascinating and enlightening practice. By learning to quiet the mind and access the subconscious, we can expand our awareness and tap into a greater understanding of the world around us.

Chapter 25: Telepathy

Have you ever had a thought or feeling that seemed to come out of nowhere, only to find out that someone else was thinking the same thing? Or have you ever had a strong urge to call or text someone, only to find out that they were just thinking about you? These experiences might be a form of telepathy, a psychic ability that allows individuals to communicate through thoughts and emotions without the need for physical communication. In this chapter, we will explore what telepathy is, its history, and techniques for developing this fascinating ability.

What is Telepathy?

Telepathy is a psychic ability that allows individuals to communicate through thoughts and emotions. It is also known as mind-to-mind communication or mental telepathy. Telepathy can occur spontaneously, but it can also be developed and practiced with training.

Telepathy can take many forms. It can involve the transmission of words, images, emotions, or sensations. It can be a two-way communication, or it can be a one-way transmission from one individual to another. Telepathy can also occur between animals and humans, or between humans and non-human entities.

Telepathy has been studied extensively by scientists and parapsychologists, but its existence is still debated by some. Skeptics argue that telepathy is nothing more than coincidence, selective memory, or wishful thinking. However, many individuals and researchers believe that telepathy is a real and natural human ability that has yet to be fully understood.

Techniques for Developing Telepathy

Telepathy is a natural ability that everyone possesses to some extent. However, like any skill, it can be developed and improved with practice. Here are some techniques for developing telepathy:

Meditation

Meditation is a powerful tool for developing telepathy. It helps to quiet the mind and access the subconscious, which is where telepathic communication often occurs. To meditate, find a quiet and comfortable place where you won't be disturbed. Sit or lie down and close your eyes. Focus on your breath and allow your thoughts to come and go without judgment. If a thought or feeling arises, acknowledge it and let it pass. With practice, you will be able to quiet your mind and access your subconscious more easily.

Visualization

Visualization is another powerful tool for developing telepathy. It helps to focus the mind and access the subconscious. To visualize, imagine a clear and vivid image of the person you want to communicate with. Visualize them in your mind's eye and imagine sending a message to them through your thoughts and emotions. You might visualize a beam of light or a bubble of energy connecting you and the other person. Trust your intuition and allow the message to flow naturally.

Empathy

Empathy is the ability to understand and share the feelings of others. It is a natural human ability that can be developed and improved with practice. To develop empathy, practice putting yourself in other people's shoes. Imagine what it would be like to experience their thoughts and emotions. Pay attention to your own thoughts and emotions, as they can provide clues to what others are feeling. With practice, you will be able to pick up on subtle cues and communicate more effectively with others.

Telepathic Exercises

There are many exercises that can be used to develop telepathy. One exercise involves choosing a partner and focusing on each other's thoughts and emotions. Sit facing each other and relax. Take turns sending and receiving messages through your thoughts and emotions. You might start with simple messages, such as colors or shapes, and work your way up to more complex messages. Practice regularly and keep a journal to track your progress.

Dreams

Dreams can be a powerful tool for developing telepathy. Before going to bed , set the intention to communicate with someone through your dreams. Visualize the person you want to communicate with and imagine sending a message to them through your thoughts and emotions. Keep a dream journal next to your bed and write down any dreams you have. Look for symbols or messages that may be related to the person you were trying to communicate with.

Practice Patience and Persistence

Developing telepathy takes time and practice. It is important to be patient and persistent in your efforts. Don't be discouraged if you don't see immediate results. Keep practicing and experimenting with different techniques until you find what works best for you.

The History of Telepathy

The concept of telepathy has been around for centuries. It is believed to have originated in ancient cultures, such as those of the Native Americans and the Aboriginal Australians, who believed in the power of telepathic communication. The term "telepathy" was first coined by the French philosopher and psychical researcher, Henri Bergson, in 1882.

In the late 19th and early 20th centuries, telepathy gained popularity among scientists and psychical researchers. Many believed that telepathy was a real and natural human ability that could be studied and understood through scientific investigation. In 1882, the Society for Psychical Research was founded in London to investigate paranormal phenomena, including telepathy.

During the 20th century, telepathy continued to be studied by scientists and researchers, but it also gained popularity in popular culture. Telepathy appeared in science fiction novels and films, such as H.G. Wells' "The Invisible Man" and the film "The Fury." It also became a popular topic in New Age and spiritual communities, who saw it as a tool for personal and collective transformation.

Today, telepathy continues to be studied and debated by scientists and researchers. Some studies have shown evidence of telepathic communication, while others have been inconclusive. However, many individuals continue to report experiences of telepathy in their everyday lives, suggesting that it may be a natural and common human ability.

Telepathy is a fascinating and mysterious ability that has captivated humans for centuries. While its existence is still debated by some, many individuals and researchers believe that telepathy is a real and natural human ability that can be developed and practiced with training. Techniques such as meditation, visualization, empathy, and telepathic exercises can help to improve telepathic communication. Whether you believe in telepathy or not, there is no denying the power of human connection and the importance of effective communication in our everyday lives.

Chapter 26: Psychometry

Have you ever picked up an object and immediately felt a strong sensation or emotion? Maybe you felt a sense of joy, sadness, or fear without any explanation. These experiences might be a form of psychometry, a psychic ability that allows individuals to sense information about people or events through physical objects. In this chapter, we will explore what psychometry is, its history, and techniques for using this fascinating ability.

What is Psychometry?

Psychometry is a psychic ability that allows individuals to sense information about people or events through physical objects. It is also known as token-object reading or object reading. Psychometry can involve sensing the energy, emotions, or memories associated with an object. It can also involve receiving information about the owner or user of the object.

Psychometry has been studied extensively by psychics and parapsychologists, but its existence is still debated by some. Skeptics argue that psychometry is nothing more than intuition, selective memory, or cold reading. However, many individuals and researchers believe that psychometry is a real and natural human ability that has yet to be fully understood.

Techniques for Using Psychometry

Psychometry is a natural ability that everyone possesses to some extent. However, like any skill, it can be developed and improved with practice. Here are some techniques for using psychometry:

Start with an object that has a personal connection

To begin practicing psychometry, start with an object that has a personal connection to you. This could be an object that you frequently use, wear, or carry with you. Examples might include a favorite piece of jewelry, a watch, or a keychain. Hold the object in your hand and focus on it. Pay attention to any sensations or emotions that come up.

Relax and quiet your mind

Before attempting psychometry, it is important to relax and quiet your mind. This can help you to tune into the energy of the object more easily. Find a quiet and comfortable place where you won't be disturbed. Sit or lie down and take a few deep breaths. Close your eyes and focus on your breath. Allow your thoughts to come and go without judgment.

Tune into the energy of the object

To use psychometry, you will need to tune into the energy of the object. Hold the object in your hand and focus on it. Pay attention to any sensations or emotions that come up. You might feel a tingling or warm sensation in your hand, or you might sense emotions or memories associated with the object. Trust your intuition and allow the information to come to you naturally.

Ask questions

Once you have tuned into the energy of the object, you can start to ask questions. These questions might be related to the owner or user of the object, or they might be related to the object itself. For example, you might ask, "Who owned this object before me?" or "What is the history of this object?" Trust your intuition and allow the answers to come to you naturally.

Practice regularly

Like any skill, psychometry takes practice to develop and improve. Try practicing psychometry with different objects and in different settings. Keep a journal to track your progress and any insights that you receive. Over time, you will become more confident in your abilities and be able to use psychometry more effectively.

Seek feedback

To improve your psychometry skills, it can be helpful to seek feedback from others. Ask a friend or family member to give you an object and see if you can sense any information about it. Ask them to provide feedback on the accuracy of your insights. This can help you to identify areas for improvement and refine your abilities.

Trust your intuition

One of the most important aspects of using psychometry is to trust your intuition . Psychometry involves using your natural intuition to sense information about an object or its owner. Trusting your intuition means allowing yourself to receive information without judgment or doubt. Don't dismiss or ignore the information that comes to you, even if it doesn't seem to make sense at first. Trust that the information is coming from a deeper level of awareness and allow it to guide you.

The History of Psychometry

The concept of psychometry has been around for centuries, although it was not always referred to as such. The idea that objects retain energy and memories of their owners is found in many ancient cultures. For example, in ancient Egypt, objects were believed to hold the energy and essence of their owners, which is why they were often buried with them. Similarly, Native American tribes believed that objects held the energy of their makers and could be used in healing and spiritual practices.

In the 19th century, psychometry became a topic of interest among spiritualists and parapsychologists. In 1842, a French physician named Joseph Rodes Buchanan coined the term "psychometry" to describe the ability to read information from objects. Buchanan believed that objects retained the energy and impressions of their owners, and that psychics could use this energy to gain insights into their lives.

During the late 19th and early 20th centuries, psychometry was a popular subject of study among parapsychologists. Many researchers conducted experiments to test the validity of psychometry and to explore the nature of the information that could be obtained through it.

One of the most famous psychometrists of the time was a woman named Mollie Fancher, also known as the "Brooklyn Enigma." Fancher claimed to have gained her psychic abilities after a severe illness that left her blind, deaf, and mute. Despite her physical limitations, she was able to use psychometry to gain insights into the lives of others and to predict future events.

Although psychometry has been studied for centuries, its existence is still debated by skeptics. Critics argue that psychometry is nothing more than a form of intuition, selective memory, or cold reading. However, many individuals and researchers believe that psychometry is a real and natural human ability that has yet to be fully understood.

Benefits of Psychometry

The ability to use psychometry can provide a number of benefits, both personally and professionally. Here are some of the potential benefits of psychometry:

Insight into personal relationships

Psychometry can provide insights into personal relationships by allowing individuals to gain a deeper understanding of the people they interact with. By tuning into the energy of an object that is associated with a particular person, an individual can gain insights into that person's personality, emotions, and experiences. This can help to improve communication, build stronger relationships, and resolve conflicts.

Insight into objects and their history

Psychometry can also provide insights into the history of objects. By tuning into the energy of an object, an individual can gain insights into its past and the people who have owned or used it. This can be particularly helpful for historians, antique dealers, and collectors.

Insight into criminal investigations

Psychometry has been used in criminal investigations to gain insights into the perpetrators of crimes. By using psychometry on objects found at crime scenes, investigators can gain insights into the emotions and intentions of the perpetrators. This can help to identify suspects and provide valuable evidence in court.

Insight into health and wellness

Psychometry can also be used in health and wellness practices. By tuning into the energy of an object, healers and practitioners can gain insights into the physical, emotional, and spiritual health of their clients. This can help to identify areas of imbalance and provide targeted treatments and therapies.

Psychometry is a fascinating ability that allows individuals to gain insights into people and events through the energy of objects. While its existence is still debated, many people believe that it is a natural and real ability that can provide a range of benefits in personal and professional settings. By trusting your intuition and allowing yourself to receive information without judgment or doubt, you may be able to tap into the energy of objects and gain insights that you wouldn't have access to otherwise. Whether you're interested in personal growth, historical research, criminal investigations, or health and wellness practices, psychometry may be a tool worth exploring.

Chapter 27: Astral Projection

Have you ever heard of astral projection? It's an incredibly fascinating topic that has been explored by many individuals throughout history. Some consider it a form of lucid dreaming, while others believe it to be a real experience that allows the soul to leave the physical body and explore other dimensions. In this chapter, we'll delve deeper into what astral projection is and explore some techniques that you can use to try it out for yourself.

What is Astral Projection?

Astral projection, also known as an out-of-body experience, is the phenomenon of separating the consciousness or soul from the physical body and exploring other realms of existence. The term "astral" refers to the belief that there is an invisible world beyond the physical realm that is inhabited by spirits and other beings. Proponents of astral projection believe that it is possible to explore this realm through the separation of the consciousness from the body.

There are many theories about what actually happens during astral projection. Some believe that the consciousness or soul is able to travel through space and time, while others believe that it is simply an experience within the mind. Regardless of the theory, the experience of astral projection is often described as a feeling of weightlessness or floating, and the ability to see and interact with other beings or realms.

Techniques for Astral Projection

Now that we have a basic understanding of what astral projection is, let's explore some techniques that you can use to try it out for yourself. It's important to note that not everyone is able to achieve astral projection, and it can take time and practice to develop the skill.

However, with patience and dedication, many people have been able to experience this incredible phenomenon.

Relaxation Techniques

The first step in attempting astral projection is to enter a deep state of relaxation. This can be achieved through various relaxation techniques, such as meditation, deep breathing, or progressive muscle relaxation. The goal is to quiet the mind and body, allowing you to enter a state of deep relaxation where you can detach from the physical body.

Visualization

Visualization is a powerful tool for astral projection. Once you are in a deep state of relaxation, begin to visualize yourself separating from your physical body. Picture yourself floating up and away from your body, and feel yourself becoming weightless. You can also visualize yourself entering another realm or dimension.

Intent

Intent is a crucial component of astral projection. You must have a strong desire and intention to leave your physical body and explore other realms. Focus your mind on your intention, and hold onto the belief that you are capable of achieving astral projection.

Sleep Paralysis

Sleep paralysis is a natural phenomenon that occurs when the body is in a state of deep sleep, but the mind is still conscious. It can be a scary experience, as it often involves a feeling of being unable to move or speak. However, some people have found that they are able to use sleep paralysis as a gateway to astral projection. If you experience sleep paralysis, try visualizing yourself leaving your body and exploring other realms.

Binaural Beats

Binaural beats are a form of sound therapy that uses specific frequencies to induce a state of deep relaxation. Some people have found that listening to binaural beats can help them achieve astral projection. You can find binaural beats tracks online, or you can create your own by playing two different frequencies in each ear.

Astral projection is an incredibly fascinating phenomenon that has been explored by many individuals throughout history. While it may seem like a far-fetched concept, many people have reported experiencing astral projection firsthand. If you're interested in exploring this phenomenon for yourself, try using some of the techniques we've discussed in this chapter. Remember, it may take time and practice to achieve astral projection, but with dedication and a strong intention, it is possible to explore the realms beyond our physical bodies.

It's important to note that there are also potential risks associated with astral projection. Some people have reported feeling disoriented or confused upon returning to their physical bodies, and others have experienced negative entities or energies in the astral realm. It's important to approach astral projection with caution and a grounded mindset, and to seek guidance from experienced practitioners or spiritual teachers.

Overall, astral projection offers a unique opportunity to explore the mysteries of the universe and the nature of consciousness. Whether you approach it as a form of lucid dreaming or as a real experience of leaving the physical body, the journey towards astral projection can be a transformative one. With patience, practice, and an open mind, you may just discover a whole new realm of existence waiting to be explored.

Chapter 28: Integrating Your Psychic Gifts

Have you been working on developing your psychic abilities and now you're wondering how to integrate them into your daily life? It can be a daunting task, but with the right techniques and mindset, you can learn how to use your psychic gifts to enhance your personal growth and help others.

In this chapter, we'll explore some tips for integrating your psychic gifts into your daily life, as well as techniques for using them for personal growth and helping others.

Integrating Your Psychic Gifts

The first step in integrating your psychic gifts into your daily life is to accept and acknowledge them. Many people may have a fear of their psychic abilities, feeling that they are too different or too "weird." However, it's important to embrace these gifts and understand that they are a natural part of who you are.

One way to embrace your psychic gifts is to practice using them regularly. Set aside time each day to practice your psychic abilities, whether it be meditation, divination, or energy work. By practicing regularly, you'll become more comfortable with your abilities and develop a deeper understanding of how they work.

Another important aspect of integrating your psychic gifts is to find a community or support system. Connecting with others who have similar experiences can be incredibly validating and help you feel less alone. Consider joining a psychic development group, attending workshops or retreats, or finding a mentor who can guide you in your journey.

Using Your Psychic Gifts for Personal Growth

In addition to integrating your psychic gifts into your daily life, it's also important to use them for personal growth. Psychic abilities can offer unique insights and perspectives that can help you navigate difficult situations and gain a deeper understanding of yourself.

One way to use your psychic gifts for personal growth is to use them during meditation. During your meditation practice, you can focus on receiving guidance or insight from your intuition, guides, or angels. By practicing this regularly, you'll develop a deeper connection with your inner self and gain greater clarity on your path.

Another way to use your psychic gifts for personal growth is to use them during journaling. Before starting your journaling practice, take a few deep breaths and focus on grounding yourself. Then, ask for guidance from your intuition or guides, and allow yourself to write whatever comes to mind. This practice can help you gain greater clarity on your thoughts and feelings, as well as offer insights and solutions to problems.

Using Your Psychic Gifts to Help Others

Finally, you can also use your psychic gifts to help others. Many people seek out psychics, mediums, or energy workers for guidance and healing. By using your psychic gifts to help others, you can make a positive impact in the lives of those around you.

One way to use your psychic gifts to help others is to offer readings or energy work sessions. This can be done in person or remotely, depending on your preferences and abilities. Before offering your services, make sure to develop your skills and ensure that you have a strong understanding of ethical practices and boundaries.

Another way to use your psychic gifts to help others is to incorporate them into your current profession. For example, if you work in the healing or wellness industry, you can incorporate your psychic abilities into your practice to offer a more holistic approach to healing.

Integrating your psychic gifts into your daily life can be a rewarding and transformative experience. By accepting and embracing your abilities, practicing regularly, and finding a supportive community, you can develop your skills and use them for personal growth and helping others. Remember to always approach your psychic gifts with a sense of humility and respect, and use them ethically and responsibly.

Chapter 29: Conclusion

As we come to the end of this book on clairvoyance and psychic development, it's important to reflect on what we've learned and how we can continue to grow and develop our psychic gifts. Here are some key takeaways from the book:

Everyone has psychic abilities: It's important to remember that psychic abilities are not reserved for a select few. We all have the potential to develop our psychic gifts, and it's a matter of practice and dedication.

Clairvoyance is just one type of psychic ability: While clairvoyance is often the most well-known psychic ability, there are many other types of psychic gifts, such as clairsentience, clairaudience, and mediumship. It's important to explore and develop all of your psychic gifts, as they can work together to enhance your abilities.

Practice is key: Developing your psychic abilities requires consistent practice and dedication. Just like any other skill, the more you practice, the stronger your abilities will become.

Trust your intuition: Your intuition is a powerful tool in developing your psychic gifts. Trust your gut feelings and inner guidance, and don't be afraid to follow your intuition, even if it doesn't make logical sense.

Protection is important: When working with psychic energy, it's important to protect yourself from negative or harmful energies. Use visualization techniques, such as imagining yourself surrounded by a white light, to protect yourself.

Use your gifts for good: Psychic abilities can be used to help others and promote positive change in the world. Use your gifts to help others and make a difference in the world.

In conclusion, developing your psychic gifts can be a powerful and transformative experience. It requires patience, dedication, and practice, but the rewards are immeasurable. Remember to trust your intuition, protect yourself from negative energies, and use your gifts for good. With continued practice and exploration, you can unlock the full potential of your psychic abilities and create a more meaningful and fulfilling life.

I want to express my sincerest gratitude for taking the time to read this book on clairvoyance and psychic development. It has been a joy to share my knowledge and insights with you, and I hope that you have found it helpful in your own personal journey.

I want to encourage you to continue exploring and practicing your psychic gifts. Remember that psychic abilities are not just reserved for a select few, but rather, they are a natural part of human potential. With practice, patience, and dedication, you can continue to develop and strengthen your abilities.

Always trust your intuition and don't be afraid to seek guidance and support from others who share your interest in psychic development. There are many resources and communities available to help you on your journey.

Thank you again for reading this book, and I wish you all the best on your continued exploration of clairvoyance and psychic development.

Sincerely,

Sergio Rijo

Don't miss out!

Visit the website below and you can sign up to receive emails whenever SERGIO RIJO publishes a new book. There's no charge and no obligation.

https://books2read.com/r/B-A-COYW-ADXHC

BOOKS 2 READ

Connecting independent readers to independent writers.

Also by SERGIO RIJO

Rose Tattoo Designs: 300+ Designs to Inspire Your Next Tattoo

The Geometric Tattoo Handbook: A Complete Collection of 300+ Designs

Skull Tatoo Designs: Over 300 Tattoo Designs to Inspire You

Soulful: Unlocking the 16 Traits of Advanced Souls

Memory Mastery: The Proven System to Retain Information Effectively

Rise and Shine: A Guide to Kundalini Awakening for the Modern Spiritual Seeker

The Power of Presence: Connecting with Your Higher Self and Living with Purpose

Powerful Techniques for Mastering the Art of Influence: Proven Strategies to Exert Maximum Power and Persuasion

The Art of Remote Viewing: A Step-by-Step Guide to Unlocking Your Psychic Abilities

Money Magnetism: The Art of Attracting Abundance

The Happiness Handbook: A Practical Guide to Finding Joy and Fulfillment

The Smarter You: Proven Ways to Boost Your Intelligence

Appetite Control Strategies: The Secret to Successful Weight Loss

Off The Grid Living: A Comprehensive Guide to Sustainable and Self-Sufficient Living

The Ultimate Guide to Get Your Ex Back: A Step-by-Step Blueprint to Rekindle Love and Heal Your Relationship

Calm and Centered: Overcoming Anxiety and Panic Attacks Naturally

The Power Within: Boosting Self-Esteem and Confidence through Positive Self-Talk and Self-Care Practices

Grateful Living: Transform Your Life with the Power of Gratitude

Procrastination Uncovered: Understanding and Overcoming the Epidemic of Delay

Social Butterfly: Tips and Strategies for Conquering Shyness and Social Anxiety

Psychic Vampires and Empaths: The Ultimate Guide to Protection and Healing with Energy, Crystals, Reiki, and More

Developing Clairvoyance: The Ultimate Guide to Unlocking Your Psychic Gifts and Connecting with the Spiritual World

Mastering Telekinesis: A Step-by-Step Guide to Developing Your Psychokinetic Abilities

Afterlife: Understanding Signs and Communication from Deceased Loved Ones

Navigating Spiritual Depression: Finding Meaning in the Dark Night of the Soul

Journey of the Old Soul: Navigating Life with Empathy, Wisdom, and Purpose

Third Eye Awakening: A Comprehensive Guide to Unlocking Your Inner Vision, Enhancing Intuition, and Activating the Pineal Gland for Spiritual Insight and Heightened Perception

Telepathy Unveiled: A Journey into the Secrets of Sending Telepathic Messages and Psychic Development

44 Letters from God: Divine Guidance for Life's Journey

Mastering Emotional Intelligence: Strategies for Cultivating Self-Awareness, Self-Regulation, and Empathy

The Power of Solitude: Embracing Alone Time for Self-Discovery and Fulfillment

The Ultimate Guide to Beekeeping: Tips and Tricks for Beginners

Akashic Records and Past Lives: Understanding How Past Lives Can Impact Your Present and Future

Mindful Eating for Emotional Freedom: Break the Cycle of Emotional Eating Habits

Stand-Up Comedy: A Guide to Writing and Performing with Confidence

The Art of Budget Travel: Techniques for Saving Money and Maximizing Experiences While Traveling

The Mystic Art of Alchemy: Understanding the Symbolism and Practice of Spiritual Transformation

The Power Within: A Guide to Self-Healing with Energy
Solo Travel: Techniques for Planning and Executing a Successful Solo Trip
The Art of Extreme Budgeting: How to Live on Almost Nothing and Thrive
The Science of Luck: How to Increase Your Odds of Success
The Science of Color: Understanding the Psychology of Color
The Secret Life of the Brain: Exploring the Mysteries and Wonders of Our Most Vital Organ
Listen Up: Unlocking the Secrets of Active Listening
The Power of Self-Love: Transforming Your Life Through Compassion and Acceptance
The Science of Time Travel: Theories and Possibilities Explained
Beyond the Mind's Illusions: Mastering Thought Patterns for Freedom from Suffering
Quantum Light Mastery: Unleashing Infinite Power
The Archetype Code: Unveiling Your True Self
The Empath's Path: Journey to Self-Discovery
Surrender to Freedom: Letting Go for Conscious Living

About the Author

Join me on an adventure through captivating stories! I'm Sergio Rijo, a passionate writer with 20 years of experience in crafting books across genres. Let's explore new worlds together and get hooked from start to finish.

Printed by Libri Plureos GmbH in Hamburg,
Germany